WHEN SORROW COMES

RITA F. SNOWDEN – apart from her books – is widely known in many countries. After six years at business, she trained as a deaconess of the New Zealand Methodist Church. She served in turn two pioneer country areas and moved to the largest city for some years of social work during an economic depression. While bedridden with a severe heart condition, she wrote her first book, *Through Open Windows*.

Her extensive travels include five years touring New Zealand, lecturing and introducing books. In Australia she was guest speaker at the Methodist Centenary in Queensland and, some years later, at the Methodist Home Mission Centenary in New South Wales; in a similar working capacity she visited other Australian states including the primitive Inland. She has also travelled widely in Europe, Palestine, the Middle East and Japan.

Miss Snowden has served the world Church – beyond the ministry of her own denomination – with regular broadcasting commitments. She has written and spoken in Britain, Canada and the United States, and in Tonga at the invitation of Queen Salote. She has represented Ler Church at the World Methodist Conference in Oxford, later being elected the first woman Vice-president of the New Zealand Methodist Church, and President of its Deaconess Association. She is an Hon. Vice-president of the New Zealand Women Writers' Society, a Fellow of The International Institute of Arts and Letters and a member of P.E.N. A long-time contributor to the *British Weekly* and other periodicals in the English-speaking world, she is the author of more than fifty books for adults and children – her most recent being the companion volumes: *A Woman's Book of Prayers, Prayers for the Family, Where the Action Is, Prayers in Later Life* and *More Prayers for Women*. Rita Snowden was recently awarded the O.B.E.

Companion Volumes

A WOMAN'S BOOK OF PRAYERS
PRAYERS FOR THE FAMILY
WHERE THE ACTION IS
PRAYERS IN LATER LIFE
MORE PRAYERS FOR WOMEN
WHEN MY VISITORS GO

Rita F. Snowden

RITA F. SNOWDEN

When Sorrow Comes

Collins + World

FOUNTAIN BOOKS

Published in co-operation with the
Christian Book Promotion Trust

First published Collins + World 1977
© 1977 Rita F. Snowden

Made and printed in Great Britain by
William Collins Sons & Co Ltd Glasgow

CONTENTS

PREFACE

Despite our human differences Here and Now, we share some things in common. Childhood, youth and maturity carry us all forward. Again and again Joy lightens up our sky; but to each of us in turn comes a time when we must walk the Sorrowful Way. It has ever been so, back to the world's first family – when Mother Eve sat with her lifeless boy's head on her lap, and looked up at the stars. There was for her no neighbour, no friend to come with comfort; but these needs can all now be met. That friend, that neighbour might be you, or me; that book to hand, this little book that I write out of my own experience of sorrow.

Sorrow, of course, is not limited to one's experience of death – though it is of this alone that this little book speaks.

As I set about it, I realize that it must be written in four parts – 'When Sorrow comes to one whom I know', 'When Sorrow comes to me', 'Prayers for one working through Sorrow', and 'An Anthology of Comfort'.

We sometimes speak of death in the midst of life; our need is to speak of life in the midst of death. And that is no easy thing where some are concerned, because one must have faith for that.

When sorrow comes the very foundations of life are shaken. Life ever afterwards is different. It is not enough then to quote half the text: 'Grieve not'! (I Thessalonians 4:13 RSV) The whole must be understood: 'Grieve not *as others do who have no hope*'! Someone known, in one's neighbourhood or at a distance, dies, or more closely, someone tied to one by bonds of love, kinship, or responsibility.

In our conversation death is often the very last thing we speak of. Even when obliged to do so, we make an effort to bypass it, by indirect speech. Noel Coward's *This Happy Breed*, reminds us of this habit; there is talk between Frank and his sister which gets round to what has happened since Mrs Flint 'passed on'. Frank winces at use of the term, but with unfortunate bluntness he says, 'Mother *died*, see! First of all she got 'flu and that turned to pneumonia, and the strain of that affected her heart, which was none too strong at the best of times, and she died. She didn't pass on, or pass over, or pass out – *she died*!'

Death is not an avoidable event – it is bound to come at some time. But we are tempted to try to avoid what we can't control, or fully understand. 'Death', in the words of the German philosopher, Martin Heidegger, 'is something which nobody can do for another.' Deep down we all know it. 'The first Christians', Dr Geoffrey Fisher, Archbishop of Canterbury, was able to write, 'in living their Christian life forgot about Death till it came in sight: and then overcame it joyfully, even when it was the painful death of a martyr.'

Death, of course, is one thing in childhood, in youth or early maturity, another thing in old age. It can then be a crowning experience. I think of that old saint with whom I had talk when he was far into his eighties, Dr F. Luke Wiseman. On a forbidding foggy day, in his eighty-sixth year, he set off to preach twice – finishing at Wesley's Chapel in City Road, London. Worship at a close – shared nelpfully, as always – the

8

old preacher took leave of those who had shared with him, and set off home. (His dear wife had died years before; his family all grown up.) Thankfully, at last, the old man reached home, slipped off his coat and sat by his fire. And there he went to sleep, never again to waken Here. Of his death, one felt moved to exclaim, 'God, the Father, be praised!' One or another of us might feel moved to add, in the same spirit, 'May my passing be as natural!'

But where there is only a formal recognition of God, or no faith at all, it is a very different matter. I find myself unable to forget Llewellyn's *How Green Was My Valley*. Gwilym Morgan lies crushed by a fall of coal in the local mine. When the grievous news is brought home to Mrs Morgan her first reaction is rage. 'God', she cries, 'could have had him in a hundred ways; but He had to have him like that. A beetle under the foot. If ever I set foot in Chapel again, it will be in my box, and knowing nothing of it.'

She does not pause to look at all the facts, or to take account of the casual failure of his fellow-miners to put props enough in that particular part of the pit. So her instant reaction is what it is – her spite against God. She must, surely, have heard at some time in Chapel, those telling words of our Lord, about a known accident and resulting sorrow. 'Those eighteen upon whom the Tower of Siloam fell, and killed them, do you think that they were worse offenders than all the others who dwelt in Jerusalem?' (In modern words, 'Was what happened due to the spite of God', as bereft Mrs Morgan imagined; or to *the sin of the smitten*?) 'I tell you, "No!" ', said our Lord. (Luke 13:4-5 RSV) One must think again – and more reasonably. Whatever the cause of the unexpected disaster, with early death, we can never attribute to God our Father a lesser degree of careful love than our Lord showed Him to have. Though nothing else is clear, this must be clear.

But lacking Christian faith, how can it be? Madame Marie Curie, who gave so much to our world, through radium, discovered this. She was an agnostic; and when her dear husband, Pierre, was killed in a street accident, she was utterly devastated. It was not enough to recognize the presence of hazards where men and women live amidst dense traffic; or to accept that unearned ills accrue, as well as unearned advantages.

If one has not taken time to think this through before the crisis of death occurs, it is well-nigh impossible to do so then. Shock and grief are not conducive to a proper perspective. It is one thing to ask for suitable warning of death's coming – as the Psalmist did – but living in the kind of community setting we do, that's impossible. Said he: 'Lord, let me know my end, and what is the measure of my days; let me know how fleeting my life is! Behold, thou hast made my days a few handbreadths, and my lifetime is as nothing in thy sight. . . Surely man goes about as a shadow. Surely for nought are they in turmoil; man heaps up, and knows not who will gather . . .

'So teach us to number our days that we may get a heart of wisdom.' (Psalm 39:4-6 RSV).

'When?' and 'How?' is each hidden from one, as an answer to the question 'Why?' These questions rise so easily in a sorrowing heart. Exposure to death is a human experience unlike any other. 'The question of the meaning and worth of life never becomes more urgent or more agonizing', as Carl Jung reminds us, 'than when we see the final breath leave a body which a moment before was living.'

In early days, death's approach differed somewhat – little children got diphtheria, typhoid, smallpox, or other such sicknesses now, in the part of the world we know, at least, almost unknown. Accidents on the roads take their grim place; or drownings in family bathing-pools, where parents are affluent enough to afford such in the garden; and in hate-drenched areas, as in Ireland, death all too often descends suddenly through bomb-reprisals; and there are as well the war-cursed lands where mass death by genocide is a grim reality.

In previous ages a soldier faced his enemy eye to eye, wearing armour, wielding a burnished lance which gave him a fair chance in personal encounter. But today death descends from the skies – and for countless civilians, too. Our overall scientific capacity to annihilate our fellows has become so ghastly efficient.

Among other changes, fewer and fewer of us die at home, as was once the case. It is now customary to rush the sick one into the unfamiliar environment of the emergency ward. It can be argued truly that when one is taken seriously ill, this is the best place, where there is at once available X-ray, electro-cardiogram, blood-supply and all the modern means necessary to meet the approach of death. That is not to have ready at once an answer to the question, 'Are we becoming more human, in our handling of the very sick, or less human?'

Once, a father, mother, or child met death in the midst of the family – a strange experience in a familiar setting. It isn't often so these days, and something valuable is lost, where a big supporting family is not present. Old and young are not much, these days, actively involved. The little ones especially are sent off to friends or relations to spare them. This, a number of those highly-qualified to give judgment, have now come to think a mistake. 'The fact that the children are allowed to stay at home where a fatality has struck, and are included in the talk, discussions, and fears, gives them', says Dr Elisabeth Kübler-Ross, in her recent book *On Death and Dying*, 'the feeling that they are not alone in grief, and offers them the comfort of shared responsibility and shared mourning. It prepares them gradually and helps them to view death as part of life, an experience that may help them to grow and mature.' Certainly, I know the effect on one thirty-year-old friend of mine, whose loved father died suddenly at home, as a result of badly-treated war-injuries of many years before. As a small girl, she was whisked away to relatives, with the faked story that 'father has gone on a long journey'. Though his photograph was later given a place in the sitting-room, father's name, and remembered activities with his family, were never mentioned. Did the suspicion gradually arise in the child's mind that there was something secretive and shameful about her father's death? Sooner or later, a child has to accept the changed family situation – and more than likely suffer – as my friend has done, from un-resolved grief, as well as from the overall suspicion that grown-ups are untrustworthy. (Much research into these matters is now going ahead.) I have just fashioned this poem:

Not by appointment does one meet Sorrow;
it comes out of the complexities of human belonging—
swift with dark foreboding – making poorer,
or richer. Who can say?
Holding unnoticed silences apart,
unnoticed contentments,
it breaks the floodgates
of one's whole being.
Easy words then slip from one's shoulders
like a slight shawl;
only Faith in God that goes deep,
goes deep enough;
for He has suffered, too,
and alone knows how to heal,
to sift from grief
eternal victory,
eternal gain.   R.F.S.

1. 'When Sorrow comes to one whom I know'

The phone rings, or the daily newspaper comes bearing among the death-notices, a familiar name. Immediately, one is moved to offer 'comfort'. (I put the word in inverted commas, to give us time to turn it over.)

The word itself, up through the long centuries, has been one of the most beautiful and beloved names of God: 'God of all comfort'. Men and women like ourselves have carried it forward from the Old Testament. '"Comfort, comfort my people," says your God.' (Isaiah 40:1 RSV)

Literally, to 'comfort', means to 'strengthen, and fortify mind and spirit'. Though it carries a rare measure of compassion and support, too many of us have allowed it to limp into sentimentality. 'Blessed be the God and Father of our Lord Jesus Christ, the Father of mercies, and *God of all comfort*', says our New Testament, 'who comforts us in all our afflictions, so that we may be able to comfort those who are in any affliction.' (II Corinthians 1:3 RSV)

'True Gospel comfort', Dr J. S. Stewart, one of our most loved Scottish preachers reminds us, 'never plays down to natural weakness; it lifts up to *super-natural strength*.'

But this, of course, is ministered through ordinary mortals like you and me – and this 'comfort of God', if we carry it aright to the sorrowful, can be sacramental. Paul was one who knew how 'strength' was mediated to him, through one friend after another. On one occasion, he said: '*God . . . comforted us by the coming of Titus.*' (II Corinthians 7:6 RSV)

Some there are in sorrow who do not wait for another to come – but themselves go out in search of what they need – though this is rare. Margot Asquith, when her first family-sorrow descended, was one such. In her autobiography she tells of it. The company about her seemed insufficient, and alone, she walked out on to her father's estate in Scotland, where she happened on an old shepherd. He was very tender with her, and very sustaining. '*My child*', said he, '*there's no contending. Aye, that is so: there's no contending*'. She happened to know the meaning of that old word, seldom on lips nowadays; it had to do with 'striving, fighting, struggling with feelings, watching a situation with passion'.

Even in the long life of that old shepherd, things had changed – and they have gone on changing. In going to 'comfort' a sorrowing neighbour or friend, these days, one can't naturally count on his or her faith. 'Our forefathers,' as Dr John Baillie, another Scot beloved, reminds us, 'a hundred or five hundred or fifteen hundred years ago, habitually regarded their three-score-years-and-ten as but a prelude to something immeasurably larger and grander . . . It was around this eternal world that all their hopes and fears resolved, and the relation of their doings here to their destiny hereafter was their constant preoccupation.'

Nowadays, there is no deep-down, long-established faith, often, on which to build, when we pay a special visit. This makes a great difference when we knock, and cross the threshold, to do our modest best at what is never a simple task. It is not easy to command the right few words. To lay an arm across a shoulder, is sometimes as much as we can do. For even where faith in the after-life exists often small interest in it has been developed – transient, material things have proved absorbing.

One of my favourite preachers, Percy Ainsworth, in the fullness of his sensitivity, gathering up an experience of many such visits, said, 'The lesson of the graveyard has always been held to be *the brevity of life*; but the lesson of the grave in the first Easter Garden is *the brevity of Death* . . . It is our real life pausing for a moment to lay down the heavy hampering cloak of the flesh. The pilgrim goes on. When we say, "He is dead", we deceive ourselves. It is not true. Say if you will, "He has died." Death is not continuous, it is momentary; it is the immortal self laying aside the mortal garment.'

Foremost, in the handful of points I feel I must keep in mind, is the need to avoid a 'preaching manner'. That might be well in a memorial service, but a kindly visit of concern is something different. I remind myself that the person I am visiting is shocked; and I must take things as I find them. Whatever else, I must speak naturally of the loved one who has died. In some families there seems to be a conspiracy of silence, both when the patient is known to be very sick, and when death has occurred. Anna Buchan, writer-sister of writer John, had a better sense of normality. Thinking of one closely and dearly linked to her life, she could say: 'There has been so much happiness and such great sorrow, but the sad bits are as precious as the happy bits, and they all help to make the patterns.'

Paying a visit of comfort to the sorrowful, it is helpful to refer to the departed by name – not just as 'your husband', 'your wife', but as 'Fred', 'Alec', or whatever his name happened to be; to 'Joan', 'Sally' or whatever her name happened to be. If I have a close link, I find myself able to say something like: 'I always remember his kindness/her kindness to me', or 'I did admire him/her.' If there is no close link, I find myself able to say something like: 'I never really knew Fred well – that was my loss. Tell me about him!' Such an opening for quiet talk can often bring relief for the first time since Death has entered the home.

It is essential, I find, not to divert the conversation from a realization of loss. Acceptance is better — loss has to be faced sooner or later. One needs to be moved by a real concern, and sensitivity is essential. It must have been at this point that being as human as any one of us, Jeremiah cried:

> 'Woe is me because of my hurt!
>   My wound is grievous.
> But I said, "Truly this is my affliction,
>   And I must bear it."'   (Jeremiah 10:19 RSV)

Sorrow is a guest who comes without invitation; one must accept her presence. Not until then, is one free to work through one's sorrow. (This is not the same as being obsessed by it.) There are, of course, many ways of accepting death – some do it with *anger*, like Mrs Morgan; some with *cynicism*. 'You can say what you like for yourself when death comes; I've had enough of God.' Another will resort to *self-pity* – with the suggestion that the cause of his/her sorrow is something beyond the understanding of most. 'Self-pity', in the judgment of a Harley Street doctor who has come upon it often, 'is a spiritual poison.' And it is. So is *depression*. Sorrow, of course, tends to leaden one's spirit; but it must not be allowed to overwhelm the whole of one's life – one's talk, one's clothes, one's attitude to those kind souls who come trying to help.

Happily, the grand hearse with horses and plumes, and identical wreaths, followed by black-edged cards, is out.

For some, at the other extreme, death-denial is the problem. They cannot face the fact in their family or close company of friends. This is bound to lead to trouble later on, so that anything one can do to help to establish loss, will count. But it needs to be done with few words, and a warm sympathy. Postponement is damaging. Padre Studdert Kennedy, on a lovely morning, once echoed the sentiment of the escapist:

'I would there was no Sorrow in the world
   But it were all like this,
Love's banner on the hills of dawn unfurled,
   His kiss
Still wet upon the roses in the lane.
   I would there was no pain,
No cry of souls lost in the starless night,
   But one way white
And shining, wherein the feet of fools might walk
   Unwounded and unshod,
Until in peace of eventide, they came,
   With pilgrim songs,
Unto the gates of flame,
   And saw behind the sunset,
      God.'

But life isn't like that – sorrow comes. Ordinary aspects of daily loss have to be dealt with – laying one less place at table; having fewer garments to deal with on washing-day; no key turning in the front latch at a regular hour; no one to urge into the garden with the cry, 'Come and look at this!' There is no by-passing the numbness of loss when first the death of one's beloved has to be dealt with – though one may even go through the funeral as if an outsider, watching it happen to someone else. But later, one is likely to suffer loss of appetite, headaches, insomnia, even palpitations. 'No one ever told me', added C. S. Lewis, following the death of his beloved wife after a brief marriage, 'that grief felt so like fear.' Joy Davidman, the Christian writer, died of cancer. To Dom Bede Griffiths, OSB, Lewis wrote: 'I forget whether you know that my wife Joy died in July. Pray for us both. I am learning a great deal. Grief is not, as I thought, a state but a process: like a walk in a winding valley which gives a new landscape every few miles.' And the sooner one *accepts* that one must walk through that 'winding valley', the better. There is comfort in the fact that no one of us walks it alone.

'An odd by-product of my loss', added Lewis, in *A Grief Observed*, 'is that I'm aware of being an embarrassment to everyone I meet. At work, in the club, in the street, I see people as they approach me, trying to make up their minds whether they'll say something about it or not.'

But having visited my sorrowing friend, I must not be like that – he/she needs to be helped to accept what has happened.

A realistic acceptance may, of course, be issued in

with tears. I musn't be shy of further tears. Doctors, psychologists, and ministers these days, are at pains to point out to us the ministry of tears in sorrow's early stages, underlining the harm that repression can do. Our Lord Himself wept at the graveside of His friend, Lazarus. And He is still the unseen Comforter where tears are shed. Helen Keller's words ring true for very many of us: 'Our solace in suffering is that the Man of Sorrows is sure to walk that way.' To restrain from tears – as some say, 'for the sake of the children' – is a mistake; or 'because one is a person of faith, and people will expect one to act differently'. Tears have a deep ministry for adults as well as for children, for men as well as for women. Said Goethe:

'Who ne'er his bread in Sorrow, ate,
  Who ne'er the mournful midnight hours
Weeping upon his bed has sat,
  He knows not you, ye Heavenly Powers.'

Sorrow is not permanent – Joy has the last word. Writing of 'The bliss of the broken-hearted', my friend, Dr William Barclay draws attention to the word at the heart of the Beatitudes, 'Blessed are those who mourn, for they shall be comforted.' (Matthew 5:4 RSV) The word translated 'mourn' (*penthein*) says the Doctor, 'is one of the strongest for mourning for the dead. Very often it is associated with the word *klaiein*, which means "to weep", and it signifies the Sorrow which issues in tears . . . It is the Sorrow which a man is bound to show to the world and to show to God, because he cannot help doing so . . . There is always something missing in life', he adds out of experience, 'until Sorrow has entered.' Tears are more than what

21

the dictionary calls 'a secretion of the lachrymal gland'. Jesus wept over the city – its sin, its blind hard-heartedness. Though one can weep for beauty, and goodness, too.

A tear, a kiss, a grip of the hand, an arm about the shoulder, can say much. I take pains to remind myself when paying my visit, that it is not for me to argue, only to reassure. There is a time for clear-headed argument, but this is not it. It is more helpful to recall the certainties of the faith. Jesus said: 'Because I live, you will live also.' (John 14:19 RSV) Again: 'Fear not them that kill the body, but are not able to kill the soul'. (Matthew 10:28 AV) Our New Testament is full of assurance: 'Who shall separate us from the love of Christ? . . . I am persuaded that neither *death* nor life, nor angels, nor principalities, nor powers, nor things present, nor things to come, nor height, nor depth, nor any other creature, shall be able to separate us from the love of God, which is in Christ Jesus our Lord.' (Romans 8:35, 8:38-9 AV) And again: 'Eye hath not seen, nor ear heard, neither have entered into the heart of man, the things which God hath prepared for them that love him.' (1 Corinthians 2:9 AV) (It is wonderful to embrace at such a time, these clear assurances – though one must use one's gentle sense about the wisdom of quoting them direct.)

I must try, of course, not to be deliberately 'bright'. That might be to minimize a deep experience. To urge: 'After all, Time will heal', might be to state a truth; but just now my sorrowing friend is living in the Now, not in six weeks, six months, twenty months hence. Pablo Casals, the veteran cellist, was one day visited by someone surprised to find him playing one piece over and over again. Said the master, when questioned: 'My son, in playing the cello, the problem is to get from one note to the next.' And this is my sorrowing friend's problem – to get from one hour to the next, from one day to the next.

Nor must I forget to pay my friend a follow-up visit; it takes a long time to work through sorrow. Crowds are concerned in the first few days, and at the funeral, but it is afterwards that the deepest sorrow is likely to be felt. A visit then shows that one really cares. Said St Francis: 'Where there is despair, may I bring hope; where there is darkness, may I bring light; where there is sadness, may I bring joy.' And the words of the saintly von Hügel I cannot by-pass: 'Caring matters most.'

I tell myself I can call again with one of my favourite books; with vegetables, fruit or flowers from my garden; or I can call occasionally, with one of my favourite dishes which might do something nothing else can, for my friend's wilting appetite. Or I might be able to suggest a shared meal at a favourite restaurant. When I am to be out with the car, I'll try not to go with an empty seat. Caring calls for imaginative, practical proof, as the days go by – words are not enough. Gradually a new routine will become possible for my friend, a new life be built up.

On Sunday, I might be able to offer my sorrowing friend a ride to church. I will be careful, of course, to deliberately choose a pew other than that shared on the funeral day; for a start, that might be asking a little too much – even, to go to the same church. If my friend is a regular worshipper, she will want to go to her own, he will want to go to his own. There is no least doubt that the Christian Church at worship has much to offer that is 'comforting' and strongly supportive.

Even close friends sometimes make the mistake of thinking that a person in sorrow likes best to be left alone. A real need is that one should keep in touch; talking a little, listening a lot. Soon, the letters of sympathy will have all been answered; soon, one must go again about the streets, go with others to the market, listen to radio, look at television. There is a limit to the amount of privacy one can find helpful.

More than most experiences of sorrow, the death of a child can go deep. There is a sense in which a child seems to be breath, blood and bone of its parents. As a visitor, I must recognize this, though it's never mentioned. And if there are other children in the family, something must be said – and I'd better be careful of the simple facts, so that never afterwards will they need to re-learn about death. Re-learning here, above most areas of life, is so very costly – endless damage can be done. It may be best not to attempt to answer certain questions at an early age; if so, it will be wise just to leave the matter, and say that it will be explained when the child becomes older. As with early questions about sex, it is wise not to force-feed – one should try to realize how little, if honestly stated, will satisfy. That Sorrow will someday come, is a strong reason for giving a child religious-training, in the most effective and natural way. In Britain alone, not to speak of other countries, twenty-seven thousand homes each year lose a child. It is a pity when Christian friends and neighbours hold themselves aloof. Poor Job's experience of long ago, must not be allowed, if I can do anything about it. Said he:

> My brothers hold aloof from me,
> my friends are utterly estranged from me;
> my kinsmen and intimates fall away . . .
>
> (Job 19:13-14 ESV)

Nor must I overlook as part of my caring, my readiness to intercede for those going through the experience of sorrow. Intercession is not just nudging the arm of the Almighty. He knows what is happening; but He needs my concern, my loving readiness to help and strengthen. Our Lord taught us to pray: 'Our Father . . . our daily bread . . . our sins', as readily as we might speak about 'our sorrows'; we are so bound together in the bundle of life. Fatherhood is not to be identified with favouritism; God the Creator has made His world on a family basis – it is to the Father that we come in prayer, to One whose *love wants* the best for His children, whose *wisdom knows* the best for His children; and whose *power provides* the best for His children. Intercession – above all prayer – is an expression of solidarity. To know this, as minister or lay-person, young or old, at whatever stage of our togetherness with others, is to enter on a very rich experience. 'Our response to each experience which God puts in our path,' to borrow a beautiful summing-up from Evelyn Underhill, the distinguished scholar-mystic of our day, 'from the greatest disclosure of beauty to the smallest appeal of love, from perfect happiness to utmost grief, *will either hallow or not hallow His Name*, and this is the only thing that matters about it.' 'I have a son who often asks me for something', someone said a little while ago. 'There are some things I will give him whether he asks me or not. There are other things I will not give him until he asks me, for I need to be sure that he really wants them. And there are other things I will never give him, no matter how much he asks me, for I know they will do him no good.' The use of intercession is not that it will get us what we want, but that it will get us what God wants – and that is something more valuable, and lovelier by far. It embraces the whole of life, joy and sorrow, and all the common concerns. Lyn Irvine says in her charming book, *So Much Love, So Little Money*: 'Soup, I ought to say, was not the only thing that my mother made with prayers. She resorted to prayer at every turn of the way, not because everything else had failed, but before other solutions had time to fail.' And intercessory prayer embraces everyone I know in special need, in sorrow, in bewilderment, in loneliness. These are not just names as faceless as a telephone-directory, they are people close to me, and close to the Father. Intercession is something more than an exercise in neighbourly sympathy – it reaches up to God, and embraces the secret needs of those I am otherwise powerless to help. Paul knew this; and at a point of human insufficiency, wrote to his Corinthian friends: '*Here you can join in and help by praying for us.*' (II Corinthians 1:11 Phillips) This is to enter into a rich 'togetherness', with one's fellows, and with God. It is a costly thing – in time, and self-giving – but ordained to be part of the loving Father's eternal purpose.

When I find myself thinking like this '*when Sorrow comes to one whom I know*', I invariably fall back on the simple prayer my friend James Asa Johnson wrote, and was generous enough to send me:

'Let me be a voice,
even the faintest whisper
in the chorus
that is the intercession of Thy Church,
Thy saints,
for one another
and a needy world.
I need not know how much
my prayer accomplishes for others.
It is enough that I should be within
the unity that is Thy Church,
and that the total prayer
is heard and answered
in Thy grace,
that in this intercession
I am blessed far more than any other
I could pray for.

Lord, let me be a voice
in that vast theme of *intercession*
which holds Thy people steadfast
at the centre of Thy love.'

2. 'When Sorrow comes to me, what shall I do?'

One learns little by little. Early on, my answer to this question might well have been that of C. S. Lewis. Asked, 'as to *how* I take sorrow', he said, 'the answer is nearly all the possible ways'.

Each time sorrow, in one of her many guises, has returned I have found, above all else, that my strong faith in Christ risen from the dead means most – and I come through the searching experience undefeated, much added to experience. Little by little one lays hold of the adequate answer. The words which Paul wrote to young Timothy, have come helpfully to the sorrowful situation occasioned by death from air-combat, thrombosis, cancer, and alcoholism. Paul said, '*Never forget Jesus Christ risen from the dead!*' (II Timothy 2:8 Moffatt) That tremendous fact lies behind all hope and comfort which comes to me.

I guessed how much it had meant to other Christians of another day, when I spent a couple of hours within the Catacombs of Priscilla, in Rome. I had only got to hear of them in an indirect way as they were not so much visited as were the greater catacombs open to tourists.

With a couple of close friends, I stood under a blue Italian sky, and pulled the bell-rope at the postern-gate of the little Convent of Priscilla. In answer, a sweet-faced nun opened the gate and bade us enter. She led the way into a small room nearby, with its grateful shade, and refreshed us each with a cool drink. And there we waited, while she went to call the handyman-gardener. The minutes it took to fetch him, made it plain to us that we had broken in on his siesta, for when he appeared it was with his shoe-laces still untied.

But this in no way spoiled our sincere welcome. Taking up torches, he showed us down wide steps leading underground. And the centuries rolled back as we left earth-sounds behind us. We found ourselves almost immediately in that early, lesser-known burial-place of early Christians. And we felt ourselves privileged. We were given to understand how the catacombs spread extensively beneath the road that had brought us to the postern-gate, and the gardens adjacent. Priscilla, we knew, had belonged to a noble family, and out of her Christian charity, had set aside this area of land as a secret burial-place for those who shared her faith, and often hazarded their lives.

Now every inch of it underground was tended – set out in sections, as for private worship. The protruding ledges, here and there, were made beautiful by containers of simple white shasta daisies, lovingly, freshly placed, as if in chapels. And on the flat clay walls, engraved in colours only a little faded with the centuries, were symbols of the Christian faith in early, dangerous times: the fish, biblical representations of the Madonna and Child, the Magi, the Good Shepherd, the miraculous loaves and fishes, the Crucifixion, and recurring as if of greatest importance of all to those early, hard-pressed people – a reminder of 'Jesus Christ *risen from the dead*!'

And still, today, this is the greatest reality to me

'when Sorrow comes'. As Forbes Robinson, out of much experience, wrote to a friend: 'There is no "getting over" Sorrow. There is rather a "getting into Sorrow", and finding at the heart of it, the Man of Sorrows Himself.' So I have found! Words that He spoke to His early disciples, have come to me with a comforting relevance: 'ye shall be sorrowful, but your sorrow shall be turned into joy.' (John 16:20 AV) Man of Joy, He showed Himself, in a very rich way; but no less surely, Man of Sorrows. His joys had deeper sources than any other's – and likewise His sorrows. The Crucifixion had a deep effect on His followers – but the wonderful part was the fact that *He rose triumphant*! So that, at any moment, I am able to say, in the words of my friend, Asa Johnson:

> 'He is not dead,
> embalmed in creeds,
> wrapped in words that men can learn,
> recite, and then forget.
> *He is alive, to walk with me*
> *and with all men,*
> *to tell me of the love of God,*
> *to share with me His power,*
> *His Resurrection,*
> *and His Life*!'

Each time sorrow comes, I find myself able to remember that His disciples have always found renewal in this confidence. 'Because I live,' said He, 'ye shall live also.' (John 14:19 AV) 'The ultimate paradox,' as Edward Rogers reminds us, 'is that the light by which the Church walks, issued from the darkness of a Tomb. *We are children of the third day*!' This is the central reality that has enabled me to work through sorrow. I find others from whom I have learned, holding on to the same reality. Neville Talbot was one such; a young soldier in our day, a servant of the Church, a chaplain of Balliol College, a great helper behind Talbot House, the headquarters of Toc H; and in turn, Bishop of Pretoria. He married lovely Cecil Mary Eastwood. But with the birth of their second child, she died. It was an experience of shattering sorrow. But Neville Talbot's deep faith held, as his cable home to England made plain. It read: *'Darling Cecil died. . . Baby well. . . Christ is risen!'*

And this goes on being true in the experience of many others known to me – and it's a wonderful secret at the heart of sorrow. I don't know how people manage without it.

Arthur Dooley, the sculptor, came lately to a like conclusion. He was commissioned to do the traditional Stations of the Cross, in St Mary's Roman Catholic Church, Leyland. To the surprise of many – and to the help of many – he did *fifteen*, not fourteen. As an undertaking of sculpture, this was no mistake by the craftsman, or the parish priest, Father Brian Fitzsimons. They knew that the traditional number was fourteen, reaching away back to medieval times, in an effort to provide points of devotion for pilgrims visiting the city of Jerusalem. Gradually, through the centuries, the Stations of the Cross have become smaller in size, affixed to the interior of churches. Before them prayers are said. 'I would have left it at fourteen,' said Dooley, when questioned, 'with Christ dead and buried. But that made it miserable for people coming to Church looking for a ray of Hope; so *I did a fifteenth showing Christ risen.*' Unwilling to admit that it was 'in fact, a fifteenth – that', said the parish priest, 'should be the additional reminder being put up in the church, on one of the central columns. It was more, of course, than an artistic or ecclesiastical whim; what they were saying in stone in this twentieth century, was what Paul had said so tellingly in the first: 'And *if Christ be not risen*, then is our preaching vain, and your faith is also vain.' (1 Corinthians 15:14 AV)

Important as it is, I find this cannot be once and forever accepted; as C. S. Lewis said in his sorrow, 'Relying on God has to begin *all over again every day*, as if nothing had yet been done.' But I know it works! Alistair MacLean – minister of a little Highland congregation – has said, 'Today is a moment in the march of Time. *Now* is but a whisper of *Then*. *Here* is but a step to *There*. *The Lord is risen, indeed!*'

It is this faith which transforms everything. Paul speaks to my condition, when he says to fellow-Christians who have walked this way before me, 'that which thou sowest is not quickened, except it die . . . It is sown in dishonour; it is raised in glory; it is sown in weakness; it is raised in power; it is sown a natural body; it is raised a spiritual body.' (1 Corinthians 15:36, 43-44 AV)

Monsignor Ronald Knox and his friend, parting on Paddington Station, well knew this. Knox had paid a visit to 10 Downing Street, to the Chancellor of Oxford University and Prime Minister; he knew himself to be in the grip of cancer. On the morrow, his friend and host took him to Paddington Station. 'The station-master', Knox reported later, 'was so overcome that he took off his hat twice.' What he would have done had he known the true significance of that parting, one cannot guess. The last words to pass between the two men were enough:

'Well, Ronnie, I hope you will have a comfortable journey.' 'It's a long journey I'm going on,' he whispered. 'I think you're well prepared.' 'I hope so!'
It was their farewell – *a farewell without fear! A farewell of faith!*

We miss our dear ones, of course, when such partings come – and we sorrow. But I tell myself:

'Whether we are young or old,
Our destiny, our being's heart and home
Is with infinitude . . .
With Hope it is, Hope that can never die,
Effort and Expectation and Desire,
And something evermore about to be!'

What that great Tomorrow – call it Heaven, or what you will – will be like, I have no idea. But then I had no least idea what awaited me in *this world* when I came. Thomas Blackburn, poet of our day, puts this strikingly:

'Till nine months had gone
And my flesh was quite ready,
What could I tell
Of the world round my body?

It seems in this flesh
I can go no further,
So I put off this world
Like the womb of my mother.'

'The souls of the righteous', Scripture tells us, 'are in the hands of God', and for my friend come to death, or myself, this must be enough. Both that world, and *this*, are equally God's. It is enough to trust God as being the kind of God Jesus says He is. 'Eye hath not seen,' adds

Scripture, 'nor ear heard, neither have entered into the heart of man, the things which God hath prepared for them that love Him.' (1 Corinthians 2:9 AV)

When my own mother died, at a relatively early age, at the end of what seemed a normal home-keeping day, there was no time for my father, away from home at the time, or the family to gather. A loved neighbour, a retired nurse, who was able to go to her, reported how suddenly her face lightened and she exclaimed, as in wonder: 'Jesus Christ!' This was the more memorable, since she was not one to speak much of her religion, though deeply real.

Hugh Walpole was one of her favourite authors, but I can't remember her ever speaking of his faith. Looking back on his experience of the joys and sorrows of life, he had said strikingly: 'I affirm that I have become aware, not by my own wish, almost against my will, of the existence of another Life of far, far greater importance and beauty than this physical one.'

A close reading of the New Testament does suggest a few realities – that it will be a liberating experience, a state, not a place, exactly adapted to our capacity and delight in which earth-bound limitations will be done away. In its fullness, it must be as impossible for me to conceive, as for the unborn child to guess the delights that await in this life.

The first certainty I have is that I shall be then delivered from material conditions, from the wants and hurts and wearinesses I know here; what has been called 'the burden of the flesh'. I shall be done with all limitations of natural abilities, not to speak of my limited dreams; I shall be finished with the transient, and the disappointing; my daily struggles will be at an end, as will my temptations, and my experiences of bereavement and sorrow.

The limited powers of love, tolerance, humility, joy
that I have developed through the years, will not be
wasted – all these lovely qualities that I have admired
in the character of Jesus Himself, will then be supreme.
And growth in Christlikeness there will surely be, for
love is never static. In St John's Revelation are words
that I hang on to with great anticipation: in the after-
life to which I believe I go, John says of the Risen
Christ: *'his servants shall serve him.'* (Revelation 22:3 AV)
It ties in with what I know of His teaching of the talents.
I cannot, of course, know exactly what that service will
be – Tennyson, by faith, hints that it will be an enter-
prise 'as suits the full-grown energies of Heaven'.
Though still vague, that may be as much as I can know
here. There, one by one – says Rupert Brooke – we shall:

> 'Spend in pure converse our Eternal day;
>   Think each to each, immediately wise;
> Learn all we lacked before; hear, know and say
>   What this tumultuous body now denies;
> And feel, who have laid our groping hands away,
>   And see, no longer blinded by our eyes.'

With my limitations of the moment, one statement is
as likely to embrace truth, as the other. It is not a life,
I believe, to be measured in length; but in greater
depth. And I find Dr John Baillie underlining this
point of my faith. 'The primary reference', he says, 'is
always qualitative.' If Love is the beginning and end of
all, as I believe it is, Paul's summing-up, in his greatest
words, stands: *'Now I know in part; but then shall I know
even as also I am known.'* (1 Corinthians 13:12 AV)

Dr John Baillie is puzzled to find one here and

another there declaring themselves 'uninterested in immortality . . . We must ask such, *whose* immortality they are not interested in . . . Some will think of a parent, of a dear brother or sister, of a husband or wife, and that is well, for love begins at home. But it may serve others better to look still farther away from the centre of their own private happiness and think rather of a beloved leader, a father in God, or the hero they have most learnt to revere. In either case let each have in mind *the most precious soul he knows* . . . Perhaps in certain moods I can contemplate my own death and say, "I do not care whether that is the end of me or not, the thing does not interest me." But surely in *no* mood can I contemplate the death of the most precious soul I know, the death of him whom I love and reverence, and say, "I do not care whether that is the end of *him*, or not; the thing does not interest me." The former might be mistaken for humility; the latter could never be taken for anything but what it is, namely treason. The man who can see his beloved die, believing that it is for ever, and say "I don't care", is a traitor to his beloved and to all that their love has brought them. *He has no right not to care.*'

My problem in my sorrow, when it comes, is that I care so much. But I tell myself there is no need to be embarrassed by my tears. A writer in a medical journal that I scanned lately, was at pains to assure me that part of the reason why women live longer than men, is that we know 'how to shed tears'. Tensions are dealt with that way, as is distress in sorrow. At any rate, when our Queen – visiting Kenya as a young princess – received news that her father had died, the newspapers said: 'She wept!' Quite properly, and helpfully, her tears fell.

One is still called, however freely tears fall, to summon a valiancy shown by countless commoners as well as our Royal princess, now our Queen. I think of my friend Emmie attending her beloved Desmond's funeral, garbed in a beautiful blue in which he had greatly admired her. And Gertrude Knevels has expressed a like approach in words that move like a strain of grand, brave music:

'Shall I wear mourning for my soldier dead,
I – a believer? Give me red.
Or give me purple for the King
At whose high court my love is visiting.
Dress me in green for growth, for Life made new,
For skies his dear feet march, dress me in blue,
In white for his white soul; robe me in gold
For all the pride that his new rank shall hold.
In earth's dim gardens blooms no hue too bright
To dress me for my love who walks in light!'

When Barbara, the loved nineteen-year-old daughter of Dr William and Mrs Barclay, was drowned in a yachting accident, he replied to my letter: 'I shall always thank God for a poem one of your books gave me–"Shall I wear mourning . . . ?"' Then he went on to say how he had just finished writing the first volume of his set of Daily Bible Readings, St Matthew. 'This one', said he, 'takes me down to the end of chapter seven . . . and that has meant consideration of the passage: "Blessed are they that mourn, for they shall be comforted".' (Matthew 5:4 AV) Later, I was able to lay hold of the words he had inserted in his commentary on Matthew: 'It is the Sorrow which pierces the heart; it is no gentle, sentimental twilight sadness, in which a man can languish and luxuriate; it is a Sorrow which is poignant, piercing and intense. It is the Sorrow which is visible; it is the Sorrow which can be seen in a man's bearing, a man's face, and a man's tears.'

When sorrow comes to me, I tell myself I must hold against any temptation to move at once, into another locality with no sad associations. Though I might move, sell my home, seek a new setting for the days ahead, it will not necessarily mean that my experience of sorrow will be any less. 'When suffering comes – whether in the course of Nature, or through our own folly, or through the wickedness or carelessness of other men,' says Dr Nathaniel Micklem, sometime Principal of Mansfield College, Oxford, in his book *My Cherry Tree*, 'we can resent it, *or we can accept it*.' Accepting it, has to be worked-out with what we have, and where we are. 'A world of difference', says the wise old doctor, 'lies between these two attitudes.' And I find Elizabeth Goudge – writing out of experience of sorrow, which so often follows suffering, in her autobiography *Joy of the Snow*: 'Without my mother's vivid presence, the place was dead. But I had to stay there since she had made me promise not to leave in a hurry, but to stick it out for a year. She was quite right. Few things hold one up better than familiar surroundings and the routine of a life that goes with them.'

To some degree there may be unhelpful associations of familiar things, a constant reminder of the one beloved who once constantly used them. But there are ways of dealing with these. At the end of our main road, an old gentleman – Mr Silver – one day shared his secret. His wife had died, and he was deeply bereft. 'Looking across at her empty bed was almost more than I could bear,' he said. 'I felt most lonely at night.

At last, I got an idea: Why not sleep in it myself, then I wouldn't have to look at it. So I did, and it's made a big difference.'

What I have been at pains to tell others, must be, of course, true for me. Shock takes time to pass, and must be accepted as normal, in sorrow's early days. Its presence must not be allowed to distress me. In a sense, it may act as a 'temporary anaesthesia', preventing me from breaking-down, as I move through stage after stage.

It is a good thing to continue the many small daily tasks that I do. Friends and neighbours musn't be allowed to do everything for me. Their well-meaning, but unhelpful suggestions otherwise, can hinder for me the 'grief process'. To remain with idle hands is not to help one's day-to-day handling of sorrow. Some types of help one must accept – the help of my minister, the help of the undertaker, possibly the help of my lawyer concerned with business-affairs and the hour-by-hour kindness of one in answering the door, and the phone. And there are sandwiches and biscuits and tea to assemble and set out for friends from a distance, who will pop in for a few minutes after the funeral service. Such routine tasks as are possible, can be one's near salvation at the first.

What I have reminded myself of – when visiting the sorrowful – is just as true about my own tears. They will come naturally in the early days of sorrow. (This is something to take notice of if one has grown up with the family injunction: 'Don't cry!' 'Don't be a baby!') When sorrow comes to a grown boy or adult, it is even more difficult than for a young woman, if such childhood teaching holds. For this very reason, some of our modern day doctors refuse to prescribe tranquillizers in

39

the first days. (There can be special cases, of course; but in the main, tears can release tensions.) I tell myself I mustn't be embarrassed to grieve openly.

Nor must I find anything abnormal in a deep sense of loneliness, of isolation, of depression, even. This doesn't mean that my faith is failing. The Psalmist – a man of deep faith, in his day – cried: 'Why art thou cast down, O my soul? And why art thou disquieted in me?' (Psalm 42:5 AV) And in verse 11 he repeats his cry, so it was no accident: 'Why art thou cast down, O my soul? And why art thou disquieted within me?' Nor is that the only time of his lowness of spirit – those words recur in the fifth verse of Psalm 43.

In the crisis of Gethsemane, and on the Cross, even our Lord knew this sense of loneliness, isolation and depression – and, to a deeper degree than any one of us humans can understand. In time, this painful experience lessens, and in the end, passes. Knowing that there is nothing abnormal in it, I can press on. Headaches, backaches, and other bodily aches can be part of it while it lasts. (One here and another there, submitting to medical tests, have found, to their infinite relief, nothing wrong.)

Nor must I let a temporary inability to concentrate bother me. Usually, I am quite good at concentration. Is anything happening to my mind? No, it is not! I need only have patience, helped by the experience of others – they have worked through it. And so shall I!

It may be that a sense of guilt is discovered on the fringe of my mind, out of all proportion to my real relationship with the one who has died. Little things have occurred, as in all human lives, which must not now be allowed to grow into a neurotic state. A foolish word may have been spoken, a foolish judgment made; but I must tell myself that all these signs of human frailty are now in the past – and having been forgiven – must not be carried into the present, or the future. This is a good reason why one should never 'let the sun go down upon one's wrath' as far as one's relationships go. Even more so, one should not let one's sins against the Father go unforgiven. 'If only I had not said this or that; or if only I had done this instead of that', does nothing at this stage, but plump-out remorse. To brood on such things, I tell myself, is a great mistake; and a hindrance in working through one's sorrow.

Reaching onward, I tell myself I must do all I can to *return* to normal work and interests. This will plainly show that sorrow has not been wasted: added to the gentleness shown in one's handling of others' troubles, will be a new quality of daily awareness. I lately fashioned this prayer:

O Lord, let me be aware –
    quicken my heart to care
for Your world; and each holding breath
    cast between Birth and Death –
birds, at first light, greeting the day
    before small winds can say
what can be said of life's wonder
    here inexhaustible:

all earth's furry things on four feet,
    knowing well cold and heat,
with their vagaries of delight
    brought within human sight;
rapt children, with un-patterned Time,
    happy with song and rhyme
and life's bright curiosities
    here inexhaustible:

all who work with moods of earth –
   who give fruits and grains birth,
and bulbs and twigs foliate joy –
   and all whose main ploy
is cast with life's *in*-door things –
   the bench, the bell that rings,
or the vast awe of the atom,
   here inexhaustible:

all with new healing skills to bring,
   all with rich songs to sing,
all whose words set men on their feet
   with News that God will meet
them on their way through Time and Space
   with His forgiveness and grace,
manifested in Christ, alone,
   here inexhaustible.

R.F.S.

3. Prayers

DAY 1: *Have you not known? Have you not heard? The Lord is the everlasting God, the Creator of the ends of the earth. He does not faint nor grow weary.* (Isaiah 40:28 RSV)

Gracious God, you have created this world, and set the stars in space, and caused the sun and moon to serve. I marvel that I can call you 'Father'.
> And just now in my sorrow, I am thankful;
> You have never ceased to love me;
> You have never ceased to be concerned.

Make me especially aware of your presence now, in this hour of my need. I am shy about meeting folk, for fear my tears will well, and I be overwhelmed. But I know that –
> Nothing can happen to me today without you;
> nothing is ever too much for your love;
> death with sorrow is not life's last word. AMEN

———

DAY 2: *Jesus said to her, 'I am the resurrection, and the life; he who believes in me, though he die, yet shall he live.'*

(John 11: 25 RSV)

Everlasting God, my Father, the calm assurance of Christ is very precious to me just now. Though undeserving, I am supported by this hope of life Here, and Hereafter.

Undergird my weakness with your strength,
Replace my fear with steady certainty,
Grant me in your mercy, strong courage.

So may I be able to move among my fellows, assured; so may I know light in my darkness of grief; so may I face tomorrow, unbeaten, certain of reunion later on.

Support me with the Old and New Testaments;
Speak to me through others' experience;
Speak to me in the quietness of this moment. AMEN

———

DAY 3: *He heals the broken-hearted, and binds up their wounds.* (Psalm 147:3 RSV)

From time beyond human remembrance, O God, men and women have found healing in your presence. Life for many of us becomes at times puzzling, and painful. I sit here mulling over my memories of days past; lingering over occasions of happiness, and high purpose – wondering if such will ever come again. Though hard-pressed, I am glad that I have not to face this experience alone. Help me to be brave where I find it hard to be brave, cheerful where I find it hard to be cheerful; support me in any circumstances, in any company. Deliver me from self-pity, and lead me to a true perspective, I pray. Keep my mind and my hands active, for Christ's sake. AMEN

———

DAY 4: *If God is for us, who is against us?*

(Romans 8:31 RSV)

Gracious God, hear my prayer, as I hush my troubled heart in this quiet place, before I go out to face what I must, today.

Recall to me clearly the things I believe;
Renew my faith that so easily falters;
Bring me again in time to real joy.

Sanctify all my relationships; support my physical energies, I pray; renew my nervous energies; and bring me through this unshaken in my on-going devotion.

Bless all who cross my threshold;
those who bring me flowers and books;
those of few words – but great love.   AMEN

———

DAY 5: *O Lord, my God, I call for help by day; I cry out in the night before thee. Let my prayer come before thee, incline thy ear to my cry!* (Psalm 88:1 RSV)

O God, my Father, speak to me as you can, in this experience of grief, that I may be lifted above myself, to glorify you, and to serve here the purposes of your love.

You speak to me continually, through worship;
You speak to me through the Scriptures;
You speak to me through human conversations.

Help me to respond sincerely and helpfully; to put away all self-absorption in my sorrow; to accept eagerly the days that come one by one.

Give me the humility of a learner, O Lord;

Give me the clarity of thought that I need;
Give me the courageous spirit of Christ.   AMEN

———

DAY 6: *What no eye has seen, nor ear heard, nor the heart of man conceived . . . God has prepared for those who love him.*

(1 Corinthians 2:9 RSV)

Gracious Father, lift me above my own concerns this day. Let me learn that your love is a living love; and that you call me to a present knowledge of it.

 Restore to me a sense of bodily well-being;

 Forgive me for my trembling faith;

 Enable me to reach out sympathetically to others. For the kindliness of neighbours I give you thanks; for common gifts – clean water, and good food; for the comfort of familiar surroundings.

 And for the love of family and friends;

 For books and pictures and music and talk;

 For the Christian Gospel which transforms all.

AMEN

———

DAY 7: *Let love be genuine; hate what is evil, hold to what is good.* (Romans 12:9 RSV)

O God of sunrise and sunset, your seasons come and go. Draw my heart nearer to you as time passes. Amid my sorrow deliver me from any unhealthy sense of guilt.

 I recall the disciples distraught by death;

 I recall Mary and the women at the Cross;

 I rejoice in their experience of Easter Day.

Let me face up to life, as they did, unafraid, showing love; overcoming lethargy; reaching out to others in a like need just now.

So may my experience enrich me, and others;
So may my speech carry news of Christ risen;
So may my attitudes bring to you praise and glory.

AMEN

———

DAY 8: *Rejoice with those who rejoice, weep with those who weep.* (Romans 12:15 RSV)

Gracious Lord, thou alone canst comfort a wounded spirit, and clear a puzzled mind. You have trusted us with varied emotions – teach us each how to live today.

Let bitterness have no place in our hearts;
Deliver us from the burden of remorse;
Steady us in the realities of the faith.

Show us each how to recognize your guidance, day by day; and when we see our way, give us courage to go forward; let your world of joy and sorrow blended praise you!

So may Christ triumphant become more real;
So may your Church show a clearer witness;
So may your Kingdom values be accepted. AMEN

———

DAY 9: *This is the day which the Lord hath made; we will rejoice and be glad in it.* (Psalm 118:24 AV)

O Lord, reveal yourself anew to those in loneliness to-day; to those in sorrow; to those in pain; to those,

47

lacking faith, who flounder in despair.

I confess that I have sometimes faltered;
I have sometimes allowed anxieties to grow;
I have not always lived triumphantly.

Show me today how to 'wait patiently' on your strength,
how to 'run and not be weary, how to walk and not
faint'. Many before me, have known these secrets, and
lived well.

Give me today a desire to listen, as well as to speak;
Grant to me your divine perspective;
Let me encourage any in need whom I meet
today. AMEN

———

DAY 10: *The eye of the Lord is on those who fear him, on
those who hope in his steadfast love.* (Psalm 33:18 RSV)

O God, I praise you for unveiling your nature through
Jesus Christ – in His birth, His simple home, His work
as a craftsman, His teaching, healing, Death, and
Rising.

May the values for which He lived;
the values for which He died – and rose,
still everlasting – be mine, in this life.

Strengthen all who witness to His Way, His Truth –
missionaries, preachers, teachers, deaconesses, nuns and
priests – and enable them to serve joyously.

So may the sorrowful rejoice;
The weak know a new strength;
The despairing lift up their hearts. AMEN

———

DAY 11: *Lord, thou hast been our dwelling place in all gene-rations.* (Psalm 90:1 RSV)

Great Father of mercies, unchanging in love, it is easy to praise you when the sun is high, and life is sweet. Help me to praise you when the shadows gather.

You still redeem men and women, through Christ;
You still teach us life-secrets He knew;
You still support us in both joy and sorrow.

Enable us to face each day, undergirded by your strength, awed by your greatness, and purity; unafraid of any experience that our daily life brings us.

Warm our compassion toward others;
Nourish our faith, by worship, and service;
And send us with confidence into the next Life.

AMEN

———

DAY 12: *Paul wrote, out of much distress, 'So we do not lose heart.'* (II Corinthians 4:16 RSV)

O God, I know myself small amid the immensities of time and space. But I feel confidence in the assurance of Jesus that you are constantly near.

So I offer my prayers in sincerity;
I cast myself, and others, on your strength;
I lift my eyes of faith beyond Here and Now.

Let me never grow casual toward others in sorrow; let me never be mean with my time shared; let me never be shy about witnessing to your love.

You have set me to live as a member of your family;
Sometimes I falter in my following;

Sometimes I am ungrateful for your great gifts.
Forgive me, for Christ's sake.   AMEN

———

DAY 13: *They helped every one his neighbour; and everyone said to his brother, 'Be of good courage.'* (Isaiah 41:6 AV)

As this new day breaks, O Lord, a number known to me have special needs – some in hospital, some in experiences of sorrow, of despair, of secret shame.
    Keep each open towards your love, I pray;
    Give each good neighbours to help;
    And keep them out-reaching in response.
Grant your spirit of encouragement to all cast down; your joy to all dispirited; your peace to all anxious and distraught.
    Enable us, by your strength, to live in serenity;
    Draw near to us as we serve lovingly;
    And lead us gently towards tomorrow, O Lord.
                                                        AMEN

———

DAY 14: *I will bless the Lord at all times; his praise shall continually be in my mouth.* (Psalm 34:1 RSV)

O Lord of lasting peace, I would surrender my brief anxieties to your care; I would turn my eyes away from earth's standards, to rejoice in yours.
    Let me never grow casual about lovely things;
    Let me never grow unmindful of lasting truths;
    Let me never forget how people matter.
Jesus noticed Nature – saw in the birds and the lilies

about His path, reminders of your goodness and lasting care. Keep me as observant, I pray.

Quicken my spirit, as I face this day;
Set some laughter upon my lips;
And enable me to travel on hopefully.   AMEN

———

DAY 15: *Hear, O Lord, when I cry aloud, be gracious to me and answer me!* (Psalm 27:7 RSV)

O Lord, give me grace today to accept your guidance as the hours unfold. Let me handle this day aright; and enable me to be considerate of others. Much attention has been centred on me, of late, so that I need to make a special effort to be involved with others in their particular needs. Some of their needs are known to me – but all are known to you. You know also the secret resources on which they have to rely.
Bless especially those in sorrow, and loss; those who find themselves very much alone in the world; those who, lacking faith, have no eternal support. I ask these things in the Name of Christ.   AMEN

———

DAY 16: *I will both lay me down in peace, and sleep: for thou, Lord, only makest me dwell in safety.* (Psalm 4:8 AV)

O Lord, this recent experience has brought me close to some people of faith with whom I have had little to do before. And I give thanks for them.

It has led me to recall days past;
It has moved me to prayer in a new way;

51

It has caused me to wonder about the future.
Guide me, O God, in the making of plans, in the acceptance of changes that have to come. I do not walk alone;
support my every judgment, my every move.

As the days pass, grant me your serenity;
Help me to get back to a daily pattern;
Strengthen me where I am weak and uncertain.

AMEN

———

DAY 17: *To the King of Ages, immortal, invisible, the only
God, be honour and glory for ever and ever.*

(1 Timothy 1:17 RSV)

O Lord, many things have crowded into my mind
since waking_____and_____and_____
I cannot readily speak of them to others; but they are
known to you.
Grant me clear thought today, in my talk with others;
in the decisions I must make myself. I give thanks for
what I know of you – through Christ; in the Scriptures;
through Christian worship with others; in this world
about me. Beyond my inadequacy, is your adequacy;
beyond my fleeting life, your constant life and care.
Lift up my eyes of faith, that, day by day, I may grow
more and more sure of your presence. AMEN

———

DAY 18: *He is before all things, and in him all things hold
together.* (Colossians 1:17 RSV)

O God, beyond human remembrance, you created this
wonderful world of earth and sky and sea, and peopled

it with persons very like myself.

I have read of them in the Scriptures;

I have learned of them in history books;

I have seen pictures of many of them.

Sorrow does not greatly change – nor does loving care, and daily concern – only the details alter – our human quest for meaning alters little.

And you do not fail any of us;

You give comfort through others;

You guide us each on the way ahead.   AMEN

———

DAY 19: *With weeping they shall come, and with consolations I will lead them back.* (Jeremiah 31:9 RSV)

O God, as your earth turns, tears fall, hearts are bereft; men and women walk heavily, even as I do at times. But I know you near to support and encourage. You are able to match my strength of heart and body to the needs of the hour in which I live. Nothing is either secular or sacred in your sight – but all are of service to your up-building Kingdom among men. Amidst the transient make me sure of the glorious values that abide; the secret beauty of the human spirit that praises you. Raise from my spirit today, I pray, the shroud of heaviness, that my witness may be natural and real; let me rejoice in the things that bring pleasure; let me find a place for cheerful conversation, and kindly concern for others about me. For Christ's sake.   AMEN

———

DAY 20: *Jesus said: 'I give them eternal life, and they shall never perish, and no one shall snatch them out of my hand.*

(John 10:28 RSV)

Eternal Father, the days seem long – but gradually my grievous experience slips into perspective – not that I can ever forget my dear one. Save me from 'Wasting Sorrow' – let this time bring to me some richness of understanding, some richness of love. Let it enhance all life's colours and shapes and sounds. I do not find it easy to express my inmost thoughts to some with whom I meet – but I am thankful that in prayer I need hold nothing back, nor fear that any least concern of mine will not be fully understood. Support me when the way seems solitary, when the going seems uphill. Hold all that is precious to me within the beauty of your purpose, here and always. AMEN

———

DAY 21: *And the ransomed of the Lord . . . shall obtain joy and gladness, and sorrow and sighing shall flee away.*

(Isaiah 51:11 RSV)

O God, lead me gently toward your great Tomorrow. This life cannot wholly satisfy me. You have fashioned me of body, mind and spirit, to live fully.
    As I draw breath here for my body –
    so I depend upon you for my spirit.
    More really than I live here, I shall one day
        live for evermore.
You have not given me to know all I would like;
You have considered my limited sensibilities;
You have asked me to utterly trust your word.

Enable me day by day to travel hopefully;
enable me to learn more and more of faith;
bless my going out, and my coming in.   AMEN

———

DAY 22: [*Jesus said*] *You have sorrow now, but I will see you
again and your hearts will rejoice, and no one will take your joy
from you.* (John 16:22 RSV)

O Lord, my thoughts turn to the last days Jesus spent
with His loved disciples – speaking with them, eating
with them, preparing them for future days.
I think of their time in the Upper Room;
I think of the powers of evil marshalled;
I think of the eternal issues at stake.
I live in a different world, but I face real issues; I put
my trust in the same gracious God; I am as insufficient
in myself, as were those disciples.
O God, there is no least thought in my mind,
but you know it altogether;
Enable me to move through this day with
humility and dignity.   AMEN

———

DAY 23: *For there is hope for a tree, if it be cut down, that it
will sprout again, and that its shoots will not cease.*
(Job 14:7 RSV)

O God, I feel often like a tree cut down; let me learn
of your purpose, through Nature – your plan of renewal
and lasting hope.

55

I do not fully understand life in all its ways;
I marvel at gradual development, and change;
I rejoice in life's fulfilment.

I would worship you with my whole heart; and serve you with all my faculties; I would look beyond the urgent Present, into the great Future.

Enable me to live unafraid;
enable me to live joyously;
enable me, in time, to enter your immediate
presence, O Father. AMEN

———

DAY 24: *God my maker, who giveth songs in the night.*
(Job 35:10 AV)

Gracious Father, I give thanks for the many whom I know, who have lived through dark experiences. I give thanks for their shining witness to you.

Let me lay hold of their deep secrets;
let me share with others, as generously;
let me make of life a splendid undertaking.

Reveal yourself today to all darkened by war; all forced to live as refugees; all experiencing hunger; all suffering, hurt, and loss of dignity.

Bless our torn world's peace-makers;
all who speak to support new beginnings;
all who teach children, and eager youth. AMEN

———

DAY 25: [*Paul spoke of his religious faith, and its reality*]
That I may know him and the power of his resurrection.
(Philippians 3:10 RSV)

O God, let me not become hopelessly tangled with the
things of Here and Now – so that I forget the Life to
come, the miracle of Resurrection.

    Amid my day's haste, let me ponder on this;
    amid my day's stresses, hold me to the spiritual;
    amid material things, keep my values sure.
Enable me to carry here responsibility, with humility;
enable me to seize opportunities to serve others;
enable me to know religion more than a formality.

    Where I might succumb to haste, keep me steady;
    where I might prove weak, give me your strength;
    where I am strong, give me Christ's gentleness.

AMEN

———

DAY 26: *The Lord is my strength and my song; he has become
my salvation.* (Psalm 118:14 RSV)

O God, you have shown me in Christ's life, how to
triumph over the deepest sorrow life knows; you have
taught me the meaning of Easter Day.

    I bring my thanks for the Gospel scribes;
    I marvel that now I can read the New Testament;
    I give thanks for modern scholars and translators.
Let me never take for granted my heritage; let the
ministry of good men and women be treasured; let the
books and music that enrich life be treasured.

    Forgive me for my poor discipleship;

forgive me for my spasmodic service;
forgive me that ever I lose heart. AMEN

———

DAY 27: [*Said John, on Patmos*] *I looked, and behold, a great multitude which no man could number, from every nation, from all tribes and peoples and tongues.* (Revelation 7:9 RSV)

O God, my Father, the concerns of my daily life lay such close hold upon me, that sometimes I forget that I am surrounded by a glorious company of triumph.
   I cannot overlook their great difficulties;
   I know they dealt with awkward people, too;
   I know that circumstances were often against them.
Enable me, in my known setting, to triumph as they did, through the power of the Spirit of Christ my Lord; and to pass on with joy the wonder of His Gospel.
   Support and encourage all others who falter;
   strengthen all confronted with sorrow;
   and bring us all in time to fuller life. AMEN

———

DAY 28: *He put a new song in my mouth, a song of praise to our God.* (Psalm 40:3 RSV)

O God, I am surprised often at how speedily days pass – out of the darkness you bring daylight, and renewal. Out of life's deep experiences, you bring enrichment. Often at bedtime, I feel I cannot attempt another thing – but sleep comes as a gracious gift – and the morning finds me ready to begin again. I bless you for the comforts of home – for meals served from the world's harvests; for pretty clothes; for pictures and books and magazines and music, for radio and television, for the post and telephone which link friend with friend. Let my life today, show something of the beauty of Christ, here and now. AMEN

———

DAY 29: *Fear thou not; for I am with thee: be not dismayed: for I am thy God.* (Isaiah 41:10 AV)

O God, I am glad to be alive, and here. I give thanks for the renewal which comes with sleep.

    I thank you for my home, and dear ones;
    I thank you for my experience of prayer;
    I thank you for the assurance of your love.
Forgive me, if I have caused anyone hurt; if I have failed anyone, in failing to witness to you in life. Forgive me, if I have been glum, or casual, or unkind.

    If I have shown a lack of patience, forgive me;
    if I have spoken, when silence would have served;
    if I have been ungenerous in my judgments.
Support any I know who are now no match for hard work; support any whose contemporaries have now all died; support the lonely, the moody, the short-tempered, the difficult. Teach us all to live. AMEN

———

DAY 30: *Thus said the Lord God . . . 'In returning and rest you shall be saved; in quietness and in trust shall be your strength.'* (Isaiah 30:15 RSV)

It is wonderful, O God, to discover that you are always creating new beauty in this world you have made;

it is wonderful that you continue to give us little new lives, to make a contribution to on-going days. It is wonderful to discover that truth is greater than any one of us alone can know.

Thank you for the words of your prophets;

for the songs of your psalmists;

and for the gospels and epistles of your scribes. You have enriched me with good parents, wise teachers, gracious and compelling preachers, authors and illustrators of books, that amuse, inspire, and support. I praise you. AMEN

———

DAY 31: [*Jesus said*] '*Peace I leave with you; my peace I give to you; not as the world gives do I give to you.*'

(John 14:27 RSV)

O Lord of Life, let me experience this gift of peace – amidst the activities of this day, I pray. I am thankful that it is not conditional on my worth.

Guide me at the cross-roads of choice;

support me in my growing friendships;

strengthen me in my service.

And what I ask for myself, I ask for my friends – in their many involvements this day; in their homes; and places of business; and worship.

Bless those with undeveloped children;

all engaged in complex social-service;

all who serve in corrective institutions.

Give them your Spirit. AMEN

———

I will give thanks to the Lord with my whole heart; I will tell of all thy wonderful deeds. (Psalm 9:1 RSV)

O God, my first words on waking are of thanks for the breath I breathe, the light of my eyes, for the comfort of my home, the love of friends.

> Reveal yourself specially to the homeless;
> to refugees on the world's endless roads;
> to those living under one roof, whose hearts
> have drifted apart.

You have placed skills in my hands – let me use them today, to your honour and glory, and for the building-up of your kingdom, O God.

> In this age of tools and gadgets,
> let me not forget that people matter most;
> enable me to show a lively respect for all.   AMEN

———

[*Jesus said*] *Heaven and earth will pass away, but my words will not pass away.* (Matthew 24:35 RSV)

From day to day, O Lord, my thoughts go back over the events of the last months, the last years – so many changes have occurred; so many impressive words that have reached my ears are now forgotten. I rejoice that the truth which Jesus revealed, is untarnished – the beauty and strong winsomeness of His personality age-less.

> Let me refuse the shoddy, the temporary;
> let the self-praising be cast aside;
> let the hateful and warlike pass away.

Strengthen all whose purpose in life is patterned on

your purpose; whose spirit is akin to yours; all who give their human powers to building-up, instead of breaking-down. In the Name of Christ, I pray. AMEN

———

DAY 34: *Seek God . . . for 'In Him we live and move and have our being'.* (Acts 17:27-28 RSV)

Gracious God, I praise you for life so beautifully varied – for natural gifts and graces, for human love.
    Let me move into this day with simplicity;
    and at night, come home grateful to you;
    I am aware that no two days are utterly alike.
Save me from spoiling relationships by jealousy, or greed, or unconsidered judgments.
    Let me not distort your divine purpose for me;
    let me follow your truth, and love it;
    let me seek your good will, and do it.
Grant me winsomeness of spirit this day, as I serve; and accept, for Christ's sake, the offering of my day.
AMEN

———

DAY 35: *They were filled with wonder and amazement at what had happened.* (Acts 3:10 RSV)

O God, I praise you that miracles are not yet out of date among us. Day after day, little new lives are born, homes are built on love.
    Keep my eyes open to your presence among us –
    the sorrowful girded with redeeming joy;
    the sinful forgiven, and made anew.

Let me recognize the difference between things real, and those that do not count; between acts of love and those generated by mixed motives of self. All Time and Eternity are in your keeping; renew in my memory just now, experiences of love and joy, belonging to the past; and lift up my eyes to welcome your wonderful nearness here still.   AMEN

———

DAY 36: *If the Son makes you free, you will be free indeed.* (John 8:36 RSV)

O God, you have given me the power to choose what I will do – and what I do not care to do.
> Deliver me this day from selfish interests;
> let me move within your given freedom;
> let me recognize my responsibility all through.
Save me from speaking words that I will be sorry for; save me from repeating things spoken in confidence.
> Let destructive criticism be rejected today;
> let self-importance be put away;
> let me deal with my fellows, in love.
Where I have behaved foolishly, forgive me, I pray; and grant to me a new and teachable spirit.   AMEN

———

DAY 37: *Be still and know that I am God. I am exalted among the nations.* (Psalm 46:10 RSV)

O God, grant me this day a vision of our land, fair as you will it should be – a land of justice, where none takes advantage of his neighbour; a land of good homes, schools and hospitals; a land of fair commerce, and stewardship of the soil. Bless this day, all who grieve, all confronted with difficult choices, all involved in accidents. Bless those in positions of great responsibility – in administration, and government, in school and college, in the care of the sick, the sad, the old. Bless all who serve on committees and boards – keep them forward-looking, fair and patient, O Lord. In Christ's name. AMEN

———

DAY 38: [*Paul said*] *I press on toward the goal . . . of the upward call of God in Christ Jesus.* (Philippians 3:14 RSV)

I live today, O God, beneath your over-arching skies. As the river flows down to the sea, so may I direct my going towards your Kingdom.

   I shall be busy today – let me be faithful in
   all my undertakings – in my thoughts, in my words.
   Help me to gradually leave my sorrow behind.

   But I don't want to be unmindful of those known to me just now going through a like experience. Let them find in your divine presence, consolation and strength, O Lord.

   Specially support those who live alone;
   those naturally inclined to heaviness of heart;
   those lacking real faith in Christ risen. AMEN

———

DAY 39: *God is love, and he who abides in love abides in God, and God abides in him.* (1 John 4:16 RSV)

O God, you know the things no one else knows – the things I am a little afraid of. Help me to lay them before you, before I go out to this new day. I do not need to ask that you will be near me – you are always near; I have need only to ask for awareness.

Let me keep a loving spirit, today;
let me keep an open mind, today;
let me keep my hands active in service.
Show me today, O Lord, how common things can be sacraments of lasting reality. Enable me to strengthen others whom I meet this day. So may we build each other up in courage, and love.   AMEN

———

DAY 40: *Far be it from me that I should sin . . . by ceasing to pray for you.* (1 Samuel 12:23 RSV)

O Father of my spirit, and of all my relationships, you know those close to me, whose faces appear as I pause to pray_____and_____and_____
Some of them are beneath this roof;
some are in distant lands, from which letters come;
some are in poor health, some sorrowful.
You know the needs of each, and can meet those needs. You have ordained that in friendly sharing, we should aid each other – and together give glory to you.
If they have problems to solve – guide them;
if they have pain – give them relief;

if they are nearing death – hold them unafraid.
In the name of our Saviour, Christ.   AMEN

———

DAY 41: *To know the love of Christ which surpasses knowledge*. (Ephesians 3:19 RSV)

I bow my head, O Lord of life, in this quiet place, at the day's beginning. Bless all who add beauty and interest to what the day brings; all who add compassion to your own. Bless all who tend gardens, matching their labour to seasons and soils, and the local situation. Bless all who tend the opening minds of little children – parents, teachers, writers, broadcasters.

Reveal yourself especially to all in hospital;
to all who find themselves in court;
to all who find themselves in prison.

And give patience and wisdom to all who come in contact with them today.   AMEN

———

DAY 42: *Love is patient and kind; love is not jealous or boastful; it is not arrogant or rude*. (1 Corinthians 13:4 RSV)

O God, my Father, from everlasting to everlasting dependable, I remember with gratitude and love all who have lived here before me, and contributed much.

Forgive me, if ever I have been casual towards them;
forgive me, if ever I have fallen to flattery;
forgive me, if ever I have lowered my standards.

I give thanks for all that has come to me through the

66

preachers I have heard, the books I have read, plays I
have seen, service I have shared with others.

I pray for social-workers, and all devoted to life;
    all set on planting hopefulness where none is;
    all devoted to the issues of your lasting Kingdom.
AMEN

DAY 43: *Have nothing to do with stupid, senseless controversies.*
(II Timothy 2:23 RSV)

O God, source of all that is true, strength of all that is
good, and guide of all your people, I adore you. As this
great world of yours swings from darkness into light, let
me rise to do your will. Give me courage this day to cast
out of my thinking all that is unjust, unlovely, unworthy.
    Bless all tied to me by ties of blood, care,
      and responsibility;
    bless all tied to me by common interests,
      by neighbourliness;
    bless all tied to me by the bonds of
      faith, and in sharing worship.
If I have taken any part of my rich inheritance for
granted, forgive me, in the Name of Christ. AMEN

DAY 44: *They who wait for the Lord shall renew their strength.*
(Isaiah 40:31 RSV)

O God, my Father, I pause awhile, at the day's beginning, to realize whose I am, and whom I serve. So many
voices claim my attention as the day advances. I would

count well-spent this time of quiet meditation.

I would recollect the mercies of the past – so many, so varied, so rich. I give thanks for my experiences of health, and sickness, my experiences of joy and sorrow. Nothing that has come to me with the years, has been without significance. Support today, all far from home, and unsure of themselves; all lonely, and without any-one to whom they can turn; all without faith, and experience of your mighty keeping, and loving-kindness. In the Name of Christ.   AMEN

———

DAY 45: *For everything there is a season, and a time for every matter under heaven.* (Ecclesiastes 3:1 RSV)

O Lord of Life, save me, I pray, from the subtle temptation to put things off – letters I should have written, visits I should have paid, words of sympathy I should have spoken. It is so easy to make busyness an excuse.

The recorded ministry of Jesus, rebukes me;

none ever lived fuller days than He;

none moved amongst men and women less flustered.

Let His spirit guide me in determining what things are important; what claims may be laid aside. Help me to see things clearly and wisely, and to keep my life-values right.

In the Name of my Saviour and Master, I ask these things – He who made so fine a thing of life here.   AMEN

———

Let the words of my mouth and the meditation of my heart be acceptable in thy sight. (Psalm 19:14 RSV)

Waking or sleeping, I am lastingly in your presence, O Lord; your love plans the best for me; and your power enables me to experience it.

Forgive me, if ever my eyes are set on distant places, till I miss the opportunity at hand. Let me use the strength of my body aright; the thought of my mind; the feeling of my varying emotions.

I pray especially for all whom I love_____and_____ for_____and_____and_____and_____ Bless my comings and goings in your wonderful world; and let me live from day to day, as a whole person, unashamed, humble, and eager to serve, your Spirit with me always. AMEN

———

Pray constantly, give thanks in all circumstances, for this is the will of God in Christ. (1 Thessalonians 5:17 RSV)

O God, Whose great nature I partly know – and partly do not know. I trust you utterly, because of what I have seen revealed in Christ, my Lord.

    I rejoice in His lowly birth among us;

    I rejoice in His home, and workshop;

    I rejoice in His words, and actions.

I rejoice in what men and women of the Christian Church up through the long centuries, have shown me. I rejoice in what meditations and hymns and the deep thoughts of theology have shown me. I rejoice in what courageous deeds, and kindly undertakings have made clear to me in this generation. Strengthen the witness of the Church in every land, I pray, in every situation – especially in places of persecution, and fear. And bring to it your victory.   AMEN

———

DAY 48: *A thousand years in thy sight are but as yesterday when it is past, or as a watch in the night.* (Psalm 90:4 AV)

Eternal God, my Father – forever speaking through the majesty of the universe, of earth, stars and plants; I love the wonderful things close about my life – the silent dew on the grass, the silver cobwebs spun, the song of birds, the pattern and colour of leaves, the sound of streams hastening on their way. I thank you for the warm and understanding love of friends, and family; for the challenges that come through reading of others of fine spirit, and readiness to share experiences. They have enriched life here for me. Support this day, all devoted to the purposes of your Kingdom – peace-makers, suppliers of food, and fellowship.   AMEN

———

DAY 49: *Lo, I am with you always [said Jesus, after He had overcome death] to the close of the age.* (Matthew 28:20 RSV)

O God, it is too wonderful that with all the universe to command, you can care for me.
   Yet I find confidence in what Jesus has said:
      that one lamb is precious, when lost and away;
      that one son, is welcomed by the loving Father;
      that one coin, is searched for, and at last, found.

Let me realize that this wonderful relationship reaches out to others – of different nationality, of different speech, of different patterns of life, of different plans and purposes. We are all your children – prodigal many of us. Turn our steps towards home, I pray, and grant us a warm welcome from others, when we come. Let us learn the ministry of gladness and rejoicing.

AMEN

———

DAY 50: *Blessed be the God and Father of our Lord Jesus Christ, the Father of mercies, and God of all comfort.* (II Corinthians 1:3 RSV)

Gracious Father, little by little you have led me back into serenity, into joy in the affairs of each day. I have learned much in this experience of sorrow – for a time the stars seemed to dim, and the way be wholly dark. But you have never for one moment forsaken me. You have brought friendship and compassionate support from many quarters – you have enabled me to recall with new meaning, many things I have been taught. I rejoice in the wider horizon I now know; I ask for a deeper faith all the rest of the way I travel – and a simplicity and sincere readiness to share. In Christ's Name, I dare offer this prayer of mine, Here and Now.

AMEN

———

4. An Anthology of Comfort

Working through sorrow, there are moments when others' thoughts can help me.

FROM THE BIBLE

Though I walk through the valley of the shadow of death, I will fear no evil: for thou art with me . . . Surely goodness and mercy shall follow me all the days of my life: and I will dwell in the house of the Lord for ever. (The Shepherd Psalm, 23:4-6 AV)

The Lord is near to the broken-hearted, and saves the crushed in spirit. (Psalm 34:18 RSV)

Thy steadfast love, O Lord, extends to the heavens, and thy faithfulness to the clouds. (Psalm 36:5 RSV)

The eternal God is your dwelling place. And underneath are the everlasting arms.

(Deuteronomy 33:27 RSV)

In many and various ways God spoke of old to our fathers by the prophets, but in these last days he has spoken to us by a Son. (Hebrews 1:1 RSV)

Jesus said to him: 'Have I been with you so long, and yet you do not know me . . .? He who has seen me has seen the Father; how can you say, "Show us the Father"? Do you not believe that I am in the Father and the Father in me? The words that I say to you I do not speak on my own authority; but the Father who dwells in me does his works.' (John 14:9-10 RSV)

Blessed be the God the Father of our Lord Jesus Christ! By his great mercy we have been born anew to a living hope through the resurrection of Jesus Christ from the dead. (1 Peter 1:3 RSV)

If in this life only we have Hope in Christ, we are of all men most miserable. But now is Christ risen from the dead, and become the first fruits of them that slept. For since by man came Death, by man came also the Resurrection of the dead. For as in Adam all die, even so in Christ shall all be made alive.
(1 Corinthians 15:19-22 AV)

Jesus Christ is the same yesterday and today and for ever. (Hebrews 13:8 RSV)

Let us therefore boldly approach the throne of our gracious God, where we may receive mercy and in his grace find timely help. (Hebrews 4:16 NEB)

The grace of God has dawned upon the world with healing for all mankind. (Titus 2:12 NEB)

We who are strong ought to bear the failings of the weak, and not to please ourselves; let each of us please his neighbour for his good, to edify him. For Christ did not please himself . . . For whatever was written in former days was written for our instruction, that by steadfastness and by the encouragement of the Scriptures we might have hope. (Romans 15:1-4 RSV)

73

Thanks be to God, who gives us the victory through our
Lord Jesus Christ. Therefore . . . . be steadfast, immo-
vable, always abounding in the work of the Lord,
knowing that in the Lord your labour is not in vain.
(1 Corinthians 15:57-58 RSV)

I tell you my friends, do not fear those who kill the body,
and after that have no more that they can do.

(Luke 12:4 RSV)

There is nothing love cannot face; there is no limit to its
faith, its hope, and its endurance.

(1 Corinthians 13:7 NEB)

And many of the Jews came to Martha and Mary, to
comfort them concerning their brother. Then Martha,
as soon as she heard that Jesus was coming, went and
met him; but Mary sat still in the house. Then said
Martha unto Jesus, 'Lord, if thou hadst been here, my
brother had not died, but I know that even now, what-
soever thou wilt ask of God, God will give it thee.'
Jesus said unto her, 'Thy brother shall rise again.'
Martha said unto him, 'I know that he shall rise
again in the resurrection at the last day.' Jesus said unto
her, 'I am the resurrection, and the life: he that be-
lieveth in me, though he were dead, yet shall he live.'
(John 11:19-25 AV)

[Said John, during his vision on Patmos] Then I saw a
new heaven and a new earth; for the first heaven and
the first earth had passed away, and the sea was no
more. And I saw the holy city, new Jerusalem, coming
down out of heaven from God, prepared as a bride for
her husband; and I heard a great voice from the throne

saying, 'Behold, the dwelling of God is with men. He will dwell with them, and they shall be his people, and God himself will be with them; he will wipe away every tear from their eyes, and death shall be no more, neither shall there be mourning nor crying nor pain any more, for the former things have passed away.'

(Revelation 21:1-4 RSV)

FROM GENERAL AUTHORS

Our basic English New Testament speaks of Christ's *'death, and coming back from death'*. But it is so much more. As Christians, we do not merely declare that He *survived* death – but that He *conquered death.* 'Death is swallowed up in victory!' It is something more than a piece of religious comfort to speak softly when the blinds are drawn; or a pious hope that will look well on a card of sympathy, if printed in Olde Englyshe lettering. Put to sorrow's utmost test, it shows itself for a triumphant reality. (R.F.S.)

'Christ the Lord is risen today;
   Hallelujah!
Sons of men and angels say:
   Hallelujah!
Raise your joys and triumphs high:
   Hallelujah!
Sing, ye heavens; thou earth, reply:
   Hallelujah!'

(Charles Wesley)

Arnold Toynbee, Master of History, sums up the centuries. 'At the final ordeal of death few even of those would-be saviour gods have dared to put their title to the test of plunging into the icy river. And, now, as we stand and gaze with our eyes fixed upon the farther shore, *a single Figure rises from the flood*, and straightway fills the whole horizon. There is the Saviour . . . !'

'I loved my mother deeply, [said one, lately] as I am sure that she loved me; but we are Scotswomen, undemonstrative, sparing of words as of caresses, and there were many things we understood but never said aloud . . .

"Nothing out of the ordinary," you will say. "There must be thousands of others like her." Of course there are, but she is in my heart and mind constantly just now, because she died just six weeks ago. These memories on which I dwell with love and pride are the things which are bearing me up, and dulling the ache of separation; these thoughts, and two things which were said to me when she died.

'One was said by the minister during the funeral service. The little church was crowded with friends and neighbours of hers, as he spoke of her life in the village, and the sense of loss felt by all. "But", he said, "there is just no point in saying we are Christians if we do not act as Christians. There is no point in saying that we believe in the Resurrection . . . if we do not live as if we believe it."

'The other was said to me by my four-year-old son. On the morning when we heard the news of her death, I had told the two older children before they left for school, and they had cried a little, and had been comforted and had gone away discussing soberly what life without Granny would be like. But the youngest was puzzled, and came and sat on my knee to have it explained to him.

'When at last he understood, he mopped his wet eyes with a rather soggy handkerchief, and smiled, struck by a wonderful idea. "Golly!" he said, "won't it be super for Jesus!" '   (Anon)

'What though my joys and comforts die,
    The Lord, my Saviour liveth!
What though the darkness gather round,
    Songs in the night He giveth!'
                    ('Praise', by Robert Lowry)

Some time ago an English publishing house put out a book, *If I could preach only once*. The purpose of its author was to list the things which seemed to him to matter most. One distinguished Catholic man-of-letters replied: 'If I had only one sermon to preach, it would be against fear.'

The words 'Fear not!' keep recurring in our New Testament.

To the father of the Forerunner of Jesus: 'Fear not Zacharias.' (Luke 1:13 AV)

To Mary, the village maiden, chosen mother: 'Fear not Mary!' (Luke 1:30 AV)

To the waiting shepherds, told of the Birth of the Babe: 'Fear not!' (Luke 2:10 AV)

To Jairus, with news of death in his home, 'Fear not!' (Luke 8:50 AV)

To Christ's close disciples: 'Fear not, little flock!'
                    (Luke 12:32 AV)

'People talk to me with long faces.
"Your father is dead? How is your mother?
How sad!"

How gladly
My father gave up all he had,
Quietly, in love, to stranger and friend,
To his own there was no end of his giving.

Please don't talk to me with long faces.
My father lives on in radiant joy,
So clear,
Not fearing,
We will, in our turn, embrace death;
Eager to taste of that joy in living.

How blind to heaven
Are those who talk to me with long faces.'

(Anon)

Epitaphs have often little to say to a heart that is in
sorrow; but a glorious exception is one in Liverpool
Cathedral. I stood reading it over and over: 'Here lies
in honour all that could die of a pioneer of ortho-
paedics, Sir Robert Jones.' *All that could die!* (R.F.S.)

This week the post brought me a letter I was moved to
receive. It harked back to a passage in one of my books,
wherein I quoted from my newspaper.

'A dying boy', it said, 'walked yesterday along the
enchanted path trodden by Christopher Robin. More
than anything, he had wanted to see the Changing of
the Guard at Buckingham Palace.

'But there had seemed no hope of it. London was far
away from his home in Weymouth, Dorset, and there
was little time. For the boy, Jamie Cannock, aged four,
has leukemia. Almost a year ago the doctors said he
might not live more than twelve months.

'Then the newspaper told the story. Colonel Sir

Roderick Brinkman, late of the Grenadier Guards, arranged for Jamie and his family to be admitted to Wellington Barracks.

'The St John Ambulance came into action and got Jamie and his family to London and back. A sweep of the sentry's arm and they were through the gates.' (I will not take space to tell of all the wonderful events of that day, though it was all in the newspaper.) 'Waiting on the steps was Regimental Quartermaster-Sergeant W. Cheshire. Hand in hand they walked into the entrance hall, the little boy and the six-foot soldier in scarlet coat and bearskin hat . . . There were lots of things to see in the barracks . . . By then the Irish Guards were assembling. They bent down to talk to him. They squatted on their heels and tried a bearskin on his small head . . . The soldiers gave him one of their cap badges. And then he was driven to the Palace gates to see the Changing of the Guard, just like Christopher Robin. Back in Weymouth,' the report said, 'before Jamie dropped off to sleep, his mother read him the story of Christopher Robin and Alice. And the little boy rubbed his sleepy eyes after the greatest day in his life.'

The letter this week, began: 'This is a long overdue "thank-you letter" for the chapter special to us in *As Fresh as a Daisy. I am Jamie's mother*. I have greatly loved and appreciated your books, and you can imagine my mother's joy at finding our chapter. If he had lived, this would have been his birthday . . . Events during Jamie's illness, and after his death, have led us to a real faith, and membership in the Church . . . God bless your pen.'

'Sorrow is the price of love,' says Dr William Barclay in his book *Testament of Faith*. 'I believe in the Life to come, not because of the proofs of the philosophers, but because the whole teaching of the New Testament is based on the assumption that there is Life after Death.'

A TRIBUTE

He was my father, and in a rare way,
friend of all about
in the quiet community of his day;
a neighbourly man,
when trees shouted in gales,
or sickness came.

Write these words for one with few words to spare,
whose hands spoke for him –
ready at any hour his skills to share –
a neighbourly man,
if birds or beasts had need,
or days were long.

As each season came with its brief embrace,
he welcomed its gifts
made known among all in that well-loved place;
a neighbourly man,
where grass and gardens
rejoiced the heart.

In Sorrow and Joy, all trusted his aid,
and his country fun,
till the day came his old body was laid –
a neighbourly man –
amongst the Living,
his long sharing through.   (R.F.S.)

Said one of death: 'I have slipped away into the next room. I am I, and you are you. Whatever we were to each other, that we are still. Call me by my old familiar name, speak to me in the easy way which you always used. *Put no differences into your tone; wear no forced air of solemnity in Sorrow.*' (Bishop Henry Scott Holland)

'There is no sorrow, Lord, too light
    To bring in prayer to Thee;
Nor is there any care too slight
    To wake Thy sympathy.

Thou who hast trod the thorny road
    Wilt share each small distress;
The love which bore the greater load
    Will not refuse the less.'
                    (Hymn by Jane Crewdson)

Benson said of Lady Sandhurst, daughter of Matthew Arnold: 'The surface of Life never lost its brightness for her. She had her share of sorrows . . . But she found "treats" everywhere, small entrancing surprises – the conduct of the ducks on the Serpentine . . . a barrel-organ of the old type . . . the Changing of the Guard . . . traffic lights . . . the passing of an aeroplane.'

'God . . . giveth us richly all things to enjoy,' said Paul to young Timothy in the first Christian century. (I Timothy 6:17 AV) This is a truth that one needs at all times to realize. Paul's first verb occasions no surprise– God is not only the centre, but the source of our life. It is the last verb that surprises us most. I once heard it misread in public: 'God . . . giveth us richly all things to *endure*'. But the word is not 'endure', it's 'enjoy'. The reader either needed new spectacles, or he stood to read in a bad light. 'God . . . giveth us richly all things to enjoy!' (R.F.S.)

One of the shortest hymns in my book – and a spirited favourite, declares in dark days and joyous –
> 'This, this is the God we adore,
>   Our faithful, unchangeable Friend;
> Whose love is as great as His power,
>   And neither knows measure nor end.
>
> 'Tis Jesus, the first and the last,
>   Whose Spirit shall guide us safe home;
> We'll praise Him for all that is past,
>   And trust Him for all that's to come.'
> (Joseph Hart, *The Methodist Hymn Book*)

Once, when the distinguished British journalist Hugh Redwood was to address a gathering at some distance from home, his host arranged for him to have a rest upstairs, before he spoke. A bright fire was burning, and an easy chair stood by. Beside it on a little table, a bible lay opened at Psalm 59:10 (AV) The word 'prevent' in that passage, is of course, the old word meaning 'to go before'. Beside that verse, someone understanding its meaning in the deepest sense, had pencilled a striking translation: 'God, in His loving-kindness, shall meet me at every corner.'

One's 'working through sorrow' is not a process of forgetting some things, so much as *a process of remembering some things*. (R.F.S.)

Said Rupert Brooke – too soon to meet Death –
   Safe shall be my going,
 Secretly armed against Death's endeavour;
 Safe though all safety's lost; safe where men fall;
   And if these poor limbs die, safest of all.

God's world is conceived in hope. Dawn follows darkness, Spring follows the leaf-strewn way of Winter, the
world is born anew in every little child, the Resurrection lies just beyond what we call death. (R.F.S.)

'Heaven, even though *there are no earthly words to describe it*,
is ever present in the minds of the inspired writers. The
words of Paul succinctly describe their common con-
viction: "I reckon that the sufferings of this present
time are not worthy to be compared with the glory
which shall be revealed in us." '

(J. B. Phillips – translator)

Said vital Archbishop William Temple shortly before
his early and lamented death: 'There is nothing in the
world of which I feel so certain.' (Speaking of the life
beyond this.) 'I have no idea what it will be like, and I
am glad that I have not, as I am sure it would be
wrong. I do not want it for myself as mere continuance,
but I want it for my understanding of life . . . "God is
love" appears to me nonsense in view of the world He
has made, *if there is no other.*'

'Sometimes when I am far from home', once said my
first editor, Dr Leslie Church, 'and beginning a return
journey, the way seems long, the night dark and my
body weary. With sudden anxiety I wonder whether I

have forgotten my key. Then I remember it does not really matter. When the last mile is ended, and I reach the outer gate, someone who has been waiting and listening will know. As I go up those few steps to the door, locked and uninviting – suddenly the door will be *opened from the inside*, for someone who waits, cares. I shall cross the threshold into the light and happiness of home.

'If God be Father, will He do less?'

'Among the influences of my life', says Professor David Cairns, of Christ's College, Aberdeen, 'perhaps the greatest has been that of my father, for my mother died when I was a child. When my sister and I were small, our father told us the story of Jesus, as we looked with him on Sunday evenings at William Hole's pictures of the life of Christ. And as a result, when I read today the wonderful words and acts of Jesus, I can still see those pictures in my mind's eye. Through our great family bereavement, my father's belief was deepened and strengthened, so that in later years he was able to help many other people through difficulties to faith. During nearly all the time of which I have memory, he was a teacher of theology to divinity students. When I heard him speak about God and Christ, and that God was far greater and more loving and generous than our highest thoughts of Him, there was an answer in my heart to what he said, not just because he was my father who said those things, but because there was in me an inner witness to their truth.

'His whole faith was that we trust God far too little, and that He has infinite resources of power and love to help men who are trying to live as Christ's disciples. As I grew up, I was to see that faith, which had won the victory over great suffering, grow riper and fuller. It seemed to make my father's spirit grow younger as his body grew older. And in the last days of his life it shone out unforgettably for those who were with him. He said to me a few days before he died: "*There is real Life and Love coming, so let's be thankful.*" '

'This world is not a marble which has slipped out of God's pocket, but a round globe which He loves, in His hands.' (Dr Halford Luccock)

Ellen Terry had these lines placed in her Will:
> 'No funeral gloom, my dears, when I
>   am gone,
> Corpse-gazing, tears, dark raiment, graveyard grim-
>   ness,
> Think of me as withdrawn into the dimness,
> Yours still, you mine. Remember all
>   the best
> Of our past moments, and forget the rest,
> And so, to where I wait, *come gently on.*'

'We are not here to be beaten. We are here, the weakest of us, to be "more than conquerors". A deep faith in the sovereignty of God overthrows the tyranny of things. All which our blessed Saviour knew so well, from His immediate communion with the Father, led Him to say, "*Let not your heart be troubled.*" ' (Dr George Morrison)

> Let not Thy face grow dim, dear God,
>   Nor sense of Thee depart.
> Let not the memory of Thy word
>   Burn low within my heart.
>   (Anon)

'I am sure that He whose mercies are new every morning and fresh every evening, who brings into every epoch of my life a new surprise, and makes in every experience a new disclosure of His love, *who sweetens gladness with gratitude, and sorrow with comfort* . . . has for me some future of glad surprise, which I would not forecast if I could.' (Lyman Abbott)

'I delight in the feeling that I am in Eternity, that I can serve God now fully and effectively; that the next piece of the road will come in sight when I am ready to walk on it.' (Forbes Robinson, Fellow of Christ's College, Cambridge)

'Ordinary people, if they want religion at all, want it to live by, not merely to think about.' (Dr W. R. Maltby, Ilkley College)

'I used to think that Sorrow spoke
In a giant's tone,
Terrible with thundering:
The crash of sea on stone,
But I have learned how slight a sound
Serves to utter doom;
Sorrow can be a ticking clock
In a lonely room.'

(R. H. Grenville)

'One of the great basic ills of this age is loneliness. To meet this loneliness men and women construct substitute and unreal religions.
   '*There is the religion of fantasy* in which people try to escape by identifying themselves with characters in the

86

movies, the radio, the television plays, and even in the comic strips.

'*There is the religion of infantilism*, in which a grown adult wants nothing but a mother's arms, and makes his faith and his prayer a way of escaping reality and responsibility, and a way of evading his own inadequacies.

'*There is the religion of materialism*, in which the heart is set on money and on things, while it is forgotten that money is helpless to buy the most important things.

'*There is the religion of social approval*. People join a lodge, a club or even a church to win the approval of others. The only way to conquer loneliness and to make it creative is to remember and admit that there is a place in the human heart which only God can fill.'
(Dr William Barclay, in *Expository Times*)

'O worship the Lord in the beauty of holiness!
    Bow down before Him, His glory proclaim;
With gold of obedience and incense of lowliness,
    Kneel and adore Him, the Lord is His name.

Low at His feet lay thy burden of carefulness,
    High on His heart He will bear it for thee,
Comfort thy sorrows, and answer thy prayerfulness,
    Guiding thy steps as may best for thee be.'
                        (John Samuel Momsell)

In Eden Philpott's *The Fun of the Fair*, one of the characters says: 'A family be like a flock of sheep that wanders over the hill-sides of the earth. Some have the upland for their part and some the meadows; some live long and some live short; some gather fatness of life, some move by stoney ways and bitter wastes, but the Master never loses sight of one . . . To the last little lamb, they shall all be gathered home to the fold when their Shepherd calls out of the evening shadows.'

This is the first enduring message of the Psalm – there is a Shepherd who cares. And the second message that it brings us is as eagerly sought, and as urgently needed – there is a way through the shadows. We need the assurance that the way we have to walk is but the *valley* of the shadow of death – a passage, a transition, not an enduring experience. We need to know, too, that it is the valley of the *shadow* of death. A shadow cannot harm – the shadow of a dog cannot bite, nor the shadow of a strong man overpower. A shadow can fill us with fear, but we have a new approach even to this shadow, when we know the One who met the substance: death has been conquered. Now we meet but the shadow; and when we go down into the valley of the shadow of death, it is not alone we go. (R.F.S.)

'God of the living, in Whose eyes
Unveiled Thy whole creation lies,
All souls are Thine: we must not say
That these are dead who pass away;
From this our world of flesh set free,
We know them living unto Thee.'
(John Ellerton)

If death should end all, then human life here would become meaningless. If we were born to play a little, learn a little, grow up, sin, work, love, hope, and soon lie still in death, then those valiant ones who have striven for character and service above selfish ease and the comfort of life, were just fools. What is the use of discipline and self-giving here, if there is no after-life where all these lovely developed powers can be used. Life's noblest efforts seem paralysed. When God gave us these splendid yearnings and hopes, we believe He was not just blowing bubbles – pretty to look upon, but of no permanence. To feel less would be inconsistent with what we know of God the Father, through Christ now risen. 'To no companion of earth's short journey', we believe, 'need we give an everlasting farewell. What we begin Here, we shall finish Hereafter, if indeed it be worth the finishing.' (R.F.S.)

'This do I glory in beneath the sun
That men have lived brave lives in evil times,
Have kept glad-hearted under stress of pain,
Have fought against all odds and not despaired,
Have fallen and died exulting.'

(Anon)

'The New Testament does permit us to say, concerning the dead in Christ, that they are "blessed", and that "they rest" (Revelation 14:13) – that they are "with Christ".' (Dr C. F. Hunter, *What a Christian Believes and Why*)

'When in the closeness of a friend I know
A feeling of great peace,
Then I am sure that in the After-world
It will not cease.
In that glad moment I am filled
With awe that I may see
A glimpse of great eternities
That are to be.'

(Anon)

'I wish that everyone would read carefully what Paul says (in 1 Corinthians 15) where he develops his idea of *another body* . . . When I look at the sheer walking miracle of this body God has given us in this life, it is no great leap of faith to believe He might be capable of devising another body adapted to totally different conditions of life, yet still performing certain essential functions.' (Dr R. Leonard Small – broadcasting 'About the Life Everlasting')

> 'The dawn is not distant,
>   nor is the night starless;
>   Love is eternal!
> God is still God, and
> His faith shall not fail us,
>   Christ is eternal.'
>
>   (Anon)

Gradually the time comes to move out of sorrow into the new dimension of life which it brings to the responsive spirit. For there are things awaiting to be realized in the world about one – joy replacing sadness, care replacing casualness, love motivating one's every action. Every little child makes known its needs – enough to eat, time to say prayers, and security, and lovely truth in home and school, till close and far, God's dream shall come to pass: 'Peace on earth, and goodwill among men.' (R.F.S.)

> 'O Lord, that I might receive my sight,
> And nevermore be blind
> To the sheen upon the wild-bird's breast,
> To the glory of gold in the sun-drenched west,
> To the hurt that is hidden in secret deep,

The holy courage a heart can keep;
To the wonder of faith, the glory of love,
And the infinite mercy of God above,
May I never more be blind.'

(Anon)

Jesus felt at home in this universe where His Father undertook even for sparrows. (R.F.S.)

'If I were asked the reason why I came
To such a place on such a day as this
When even the dusty grass seems tipped with flame,
What reason should I give? The reason is
That I was weary of the valley day
And of the calm that being sheltered brings.
I came to taste the wind, and so allay
A thirst too deep to quench at earthly springs,
That, and to get *a God-like view of things*.'

(R. H. Grenville)

Whilst I was in New York – at Riverside Church – I learned of a young minister struggling with his 'dark places in between the stars'. His young wife had died. But lately, he had chanced to hear a sympathetic voice on the wireless. It was the voice of that good and wise minister of Riverside Church, Dr Harry Fosdick. And as the young man still in his sorrow listened, he found himself saying: 'There is a man who will understand and help me.' And with that he set out for that vast, impersonal city of New York, and to the church where Dr Fosdick had been sent of God to minister.

At the close of the long consultation, when he who had been so deeply hurt came out of the room, he was heard to say, half to himself, half to the young girl who gave him his hat: 'What a man! When I went in there all the stars had dropped out ... But one by one he has put them all in again!'

He was right – gloriously right! And he was wrong – gloriously wrong! The stars had not dropped out – only his vision had become blurred; like so many of us in protracted sorrow, he'd ceased to be sure of them. The stars are always steady in God's sky. Jesus found it so during the very darkest experience which came to Him. Three great facts remained – fashioned out of the unchanging character of God – *His power, His love, His nearness.*

And those three stars shine steadily for each one of us; no man put them into our sky, no man can take them away! (R.F.S.)

'And then at last, when all is done, when it is wholly finished, the meaning of all these things, the mystery of God shall be opened; and then the Eternal Joy, Everlasting Life shall break forth; and every creature shall see that it was ever tendered ... provided for.'

(Isaac Pennington, the Quaker saint)

'Life is probation, and the earth no goal,
but the starting-point of man.'
(Robert Browning)

In Kenya is a simple, significant gravestone. Its inscription reads:

'Lord Baden-Powell,
Chief Scout of the world.
Born February 22nd, 1857,
Died January 8th, 1941.'

Then there is a drawn circle with a dot in the centre – as every scout knows – the sign for saying '*I have gone home*'.

At the end of life's day, each Christian can say that with joy and confidence. So that those dear ones left can shake free of their sorrow. (R.F.S.)

The Vulgate translation 'mansiones' – from which comes our Authorized Version of John 14, that loved chapter: 'In my Father's house are many mansions' – refers to resting-places on a road one is obliged to travel. They are really caravanserais – shelters at stages, for rest. In the East, these still obtain, where modern facilities have not penetrated. It has long been the custom for travellers to send on a dragoman to make preparations for their coming at the next resting-place. It is thought that our Lord had this in mind when He presented Himself as the One charged with the 'comfort' of each spiritual traveller.

'Looked at in this way,' says Dr George MacLeod in our modern day, 'the whole text leaps to life.'

No part of the journey we have to travel singly, or together, is unfamiliar to our Lord of Life. If there are times when we fear, and find ourselves wondering how we shall fare, we have only to remember that all is under control. *He has gone on before!* (R.F.S.)

And let the final word just here be from my loved editor and friend, Dr Leslie Church: 'No man has seen the ultimate plan, but every man may discover there is a plan. All life proclaims direction, and he who looks carefully begins to see the marks of Divine guidance. Each new stage of spiritual experience is prophetic of another stage beyond and above. It would be absurd to suppose that this should end in that arbitrary line called Death. To admit this would be to say that the triumphant result of a thousand spiritual battles could be brought to nothing by a drunken motorist or an influenza germ. Surely the Divine plan is not to be thwarted by so poor an adversary. The purpose is concerned with quality of life, not quantity, and each spiritual advance presupposes a Goal Beyond.

ACKNOWLEDGMENTS

'The fact that the children . . .' and 'On Death and Dying', by Elizabeth Kubler-Rose, Tavistock Publications Ltd, London, 1970.

'Our forefathers . . .' and 'And the Life Everlasting', by John Baillie, Wyvern Books, Epworth Press.

'I would there were . . .' from '*I Pronounce Them*', by G. A. Studdert-Kennedy, Hodder & Stoughton.

'I forget whether . . .' from *Letters of C. S. Lewis edited by W. H. Lewis*, Geoffrey Bles Ltd, London.

'Our response . . .' by Evelyn Underhill.

'Whether we are young . . .' (source unknown).

'Till nine months . . .' poem by Thomas Blackburn, Putnam, London.

'Shall I wear mourning . . ?' (source unknown).

'Spend in pure converse . . .' by Rupert Brooke, Sidgwick & Jackson.

'I loved my mother . . .' by Anon, published by 'Life & Work', Church of Scotland.

'People talk to me . . .' anonymous writer published in 'Life & Work'.

'Safe shall be my going', poem by Rupert Brooke—lines from longer poem, 'War knows no power', Sidgwick & Jackson.

'Among the influences . . .' broadcast by Professor David Cairns, printed in volume 'Why I believe', Epworth Press, 1951.

'I used to think', and the other poem on p 71, by my close friend Grenville.

'If any passage has been quoted for which permission ought to have been sought and acknowledgment made, and this has not been done, I trust that the unintentional oversight may be pardoned. I shall be glad to make good this omission in a later edition of this book.

                                                                R.F.S.

THE CHRISTIAN BOOK
PROMOTION TRUST

The Christian Book Promotion Trust was formed to help meet the spiritual needs of people through the medium of suitable books.

The effects of unsatisfied spiritual needs are as real as those of the more obvious deprivations of food, of adequate shelter or of medical care. Like them it causes unhappiness, ineffective lives and in extreme cases actual suffering which is no less acute for being less apparent to the casual observer.

The Trustees see this work as a necessary complement to that which, in other capacities, they have done and continue to do to relieve suffering of the kind referred to above, both in the United Kingdom and overseas.

If you have found this book helpful please add your support to this effort by recommending it to others.

Why is the Christian Book Promotion Trust needed?

Unfortunately the economics of publishing does not always allow sufficient expenditure on promoting a book to make it possible to reach everyone who might benefit by reading it. So the Trust, a non-profit-making body, provides additional advertising for selected books which come within its objects. It is able to do this for only a few works and these are nearly always ones which have already proved effective. Some will need to be printed in other languages for overseas distribution and in various editions for people of different backgrounds.

All this will only be possible on a substantial scale if voluntary donations are forthcoming. The Trustees have provided the initial capital, but this alone is far from sufficient.

The Trust is registered in the United Kingdom as a charity.

The Christian Book Promotion Trust,
139 Oxford Street, London WIR ITD